Saving Memory and the Body of Christ

Saving Memory and the Body of Christ

A Moral Liturgical Theology

Timothy F. Sedgwick

LEXINGTON BOOKS/FORTRESS ACADEMIC
Lanham • Boulder • New York • London

Published by Lexington Books/Fortress Academic
Lexington Books is an imprint of The Rowman & Littlefield Publishing Group, Inc.
4501 Forbes Boulevard, Suite 200, Lanham, Maryland 20706
www.rowman.com

86-90 Paul Street, London EC2A 4NE, United Kingdom

Copyright © 2024 by The Rowman & Littlefield Publishing Group, Inc.

All rights reserved. No part of this book may be reproduced in any form or by any electronic or mechanical means, including information storage and retrieval systems, without written permission from the publisher, except by a reviewer who may quote passages in a review.

British Library Cataloguing in Publication Information Available

Library of Congress Cataloging-in-Publication Data

Names: Sedgwick, Timothy F., author.
Title: Saving memory and the body of Christ : a moral liturgical theology / Timothy F. Sedgwick.
Description: Lanham : Lexington Books, Fortress Academic, [2024] | Includes bibliographical references and index. | Summary: "Healing Memory and the Body of Christ defines the memory of God as the memory of Christ known in worship, in word and sacrament, which calls Christians into the life of the world together as many in one in compassion and care"—Provided by publisher.
Identifiers: LCCN 2024003148 (print) | LCCN 2024003149 (ebook) | ISBN 9781978706064 (cloth) | ISBN 9781978706071 (epub)
Subjects: LCSH: Memory—Religious aspects—Christianity. | God (Christianity)
Classification: LCC BV4597.565 .S44 2024 (print) | LCC BV4597.565 (ebook) | DDC 231.7—dc23/eng/20240308
LC record available at https://lccn.loc.gov/2024003148
LC ebook record available at https://lccn.loc.gov/2024003149

∞™ The paper used in this publication meets the minimum requirements of American National Standard for Information Sciences—Permanence of Paper for Printed Library Materials, ANSI/NISO Z39.48-1992.

*In thanksgiving
for the communion of saints.*

Contents

Acknowledgments ix
Introduction xiii

Chapter One: The Voice of God. 1
Chapter Two: The Scaffolding of Memory 9
Chapter Three: Word: The Memory of God 21
Chapter Four: Sacrament: Incarnate Memory 33
Chapter Five: Assembly: Many in One 47
Chapter Six: Church: One and Many 55
Chapter Seven: Hallowed Be Thy Name 61
Chronology 65

Bibliography 69
Index of Biblical Texts 75
Index of Names 77
Index of Subjects 79
About the Author 81

Acknowledgments

I believe in the communion of saints. In writing this book, I have become increasingly aware and thankful for the communion of saints that have passed on to me what they know as faith in God. They are saints too many to name. They include teachers, mentors, colleagues, collaborators, students, and other spiritual friends. Given the generosity of friends, I trust they understand my regret that I can only name some of the many who have been significant in forming this book that I have titled a moral liturgical theology.

My deep conviction of the social character of what we know and do was formed in my doctoral studies at Vanderbilt University. I give thanks for Howard Harrod, teacher, scholar, and mentor who led and welcomed me in the deep dive into social theory beginning with Emile Durkheim, Max Weber, and the early studies of social anthropologists on ritual, religion, and society, all of which led to the phenomenology of Alfred Schutz and the work of H. Richard Niebuhr.

In my early years teaching and living in the worship community at Seabury Western Theological Seminary, I remember with thanks reading liturgical theology under Leonel Mitchell's direction, which led to teaching together a course on sin, reconciliation. and the Church's liturgical rite of reconciliation which deeply informed my thought as expressed in the first book I wrote titled *Sacramental Ethics*. At Seabury, I also had the opportunity to serve on the Episcopal Church's Council for the Development of Ministry. In our work together, the liturgical movement, the ecumenical movement, and the support of indigenous communities of faith formed the foundation for my understanding of Christian faith and the life of the church as one and many.

Acknowledgments

My faith given in the communion of saints furthered deepened thanks to many. I am especially grateful to Presiding Bishops Ed Browning and Frank Griswold who invited me to join in conversation with bishops, Episcopal dioceses, and congregations to address our life together given the conflict of conscience over homosexuality. And I remember with thanks Bishop Clay Matthews and Bill Craddock for our friendship and work together with others in the development of the Episcopal Church's College for Bishop. Ecumenically, my journey in faith has been ecumenical, beginning in graduate school and continued with thanks for colleagues in Christian ethics with whom I met regularly in meetings of the Society of Christian Ethics, in the Chicago and Washington theological consortiums., and in the Anglican–Roman Catholic bilateral dialogue that concluded with an agreed document on "ecclesiology and moral discernment." And in writing this book, I give thanks for the sabbatical leave in residence in the winter and spring of 2014 at the Ecumenical Institute at Saint John's Abby and Benedict Monastery in Collegeville, Minnesota, and in spring 2016 for a month in residence at Gladstone Library in Wales. They offered the quiet and simple rhythm that was just right for the reading and writing that gives form to thought.

In all, my vocation and this book are born in the life and support of the two seminaries I have served. In thanksgiving for these seminaries, I give thanks to the late O.C. Edwards and to Martha Horne and Ian Markham for their support, friendship, and service as deans and presidents of Seabury Western Theological Seminary and Virginia Theological Seminary. Further, thanks to old and new friends who have been companions along the way, not least with thanks to David Fisher for the many evenings reading and discussing classic and contemporary texts in phenomenology and hermeneutics; to Philip Turner for collaboration and support in our vocations as moral theologians in service to the Episcopal Church; to liturgical theologians Gordon Lathrop and James Farwell who have informed this book and offered needed encouragement along the way; and to Peter H. Sedgwick, Anglican priest and scholar in Wales (from an unrelated family ancestry) who in our conversations together about Anglican moral theology have informed and encouraged my hope to give voice to what is central and distinctive about the

Anglican tradition as a sacramental tradition in which faith is a practical piety.

Fittingly, in *memoriam,* I give thanks for John W. Crossin, OSFS (Order of Oblates of St. Francis de Sales), for our friendship and for John's ecumenical spirit and understanding that has further informed and animated my hope in writing this book. Closer to home, this book is written with thanks to my brother Stephen Sedgwick, Episcopal priest and my fellow companion in faith seeking understanding in our life-long conversation about Christian faith in our lives and in the life of the church.

Of course, in what follows there are things done and left undone of which I am both aware and unaware and responsible for both. These are mine alone, which may appropriately make those who read this book aware of the limits of its focus, sources known and referenced, and challenges and questions addressed. To the end, this book is written with love and thanks to Martha for our life together and for her understanding and support in my vocation to labor on.

Introduction

This book is a story about images, the imagination, and the imaging of God, who we cannot see face-to-face. This is an account of Christian faith in terms of the memories of God that express and form a way of life. These memories, complimenting one another and juxtaposed one to another, are drawn together in practices of prayer and worship, in ascetical disciplines of the body and of the mind, in meditation and examination, in confessions of faith, confessions of sins, and acclamations of new life. Practices that form the memory of God also include moral practices such as care of children and elders, honoring and celebrating relations with others, welcoming strangers, carry for those in need, and burying the dead.

As a matter of memory, Christianity has never been one thing, uniform as a community of worship, beliefs, and practices that together form a way of life. As reflected in the writings that became the Christian New Testament, the earliest Christian communities were marked by difference. And differences among Christian communities continued, most notably between the early churches and the monastic communities that arose in the fourth century CE, in the Protestant Reformation that arose in Western Europe, and with the freedom of religion that followed in the separation of church and state.

Though Christians have inherited the same Bible, in prayer, worship, and the practices of faith, Christian communities of faith were suited to different worlds, understandings and hopes of different cultures and peoples, of privileged, of marginalized, and of oppressed. These were anabaptists, pentecostals, pietists, evangelicals, liberals and conservatives, fundamentalists, social reformers, and denominations too many to name.

In different Christian communities, claims of true faith have their own histories, whether written as established in the assumptions and claims of the truth of origin, the truth of the nature of things, or as reflecting God's call to a particular people. Instead of opposing claims of faith as a matter of what the future will bring, this account of Christian faith is a claim that faith is a matter of a way of life in the life of the world that is the way of love and grace in life in God as incarnate in creation, in what gives and redeems life in time rather than at the end of time or beyond time.

As argued most fully by Gordon Lathrop, the memory of God in Christ is formed in a polyphony of voices that reveals what gives life as celebrated in the Eucharist and in the life of the assembly.[1] Such is the memory of God that is the memory of Christians who claim the Bible as holy scripture. Grounded in prayer, worship, and the practices of faith, in their diversity, these voices are attuned to those who have ears to know the grace of God that is given in suffering the life of the world, in constraints and sorrows, in challenges and opportunities, in compassion and embrace, in recognition and care. Imaged in the Christian tradition, Christian faith is given in word and sacrament that celebrate and draw Christians into life together in the life of the world in love of God and love of neighbor.

The nature of the memory that forms this understanding of the memory and call of God has been informed by studies in human development and in understandings of the neural physiology of memory. Together with the social character of memory informed by the social phenomenology of Alfred Schutz, the hermeneutical phenomenology of Paul Ricoeur, and the existential phenomenology of Martin Heidegger, this account of Christian faith and the memory of God stands in the French reflexive tradition of philosophy where meaning and freedom are grounded and formed in act and the desire of God.[2]

More broadly, the works of Robert Bellah and Charles Taylor inform my understanding of memory as given and historically shaped. Robert Bellah's *Religion in Human Evolution,* Charles Taylor's *A Secular Age,* and his earlier *Sources of the Self: The Making of the Modern Identity* are what I call "big books."[3] They are the lifework of these two scholars. Deeply and broadly interdisciplinary, they draw from evolutionary biology, cultural anthropology, ritual and historical studies, work in hermeneutics, and social theory, as well as from other disciplines of study in order to provide accounts of the historical development of religion, Christian faith, and human society. Together, Bellah and Taylor have significantly informed my understanding of Christian faith and life as formed in the life of the world and in forming human life and the world.

In focus and style, this book may be understood in the terms that H. Richard Niebuhr used to describe his own work. This book is a work in "Christian moral philosophy."[4] Rather than seeking to speak within the circle of faith, as Karl Barth did in developing his evangelical theology, Niebuhr sought to provide a theistic moral theology as a mode of existence, as a way of being in the world. This meant beginning with understanding Christian faith as the response of Christians to God as the power that gives life and draws persons out into life in suffering the world as acting upon them. For Niebuhr, this life is a matter of life given in time and in the life lived in the memory of Jesus Christ as God incarnate.[5]

With a focus on memory and Christian faith as forming moral consciousness, Niebuhr opened conversations across religious traditions and across academic fields of study. He also made clear what is distinctive about Christian faith and its relationship to society and culture. In this sense, my focus on memory reflects that of Niebuhr's, although I write in terms of how that is given in Christian communities of worship. After all, while Niebuhr wrote as a reformed theologian where Christian faith is given in the focus on judgment and grace as revealed in scripture, I write as an Anglican for whom Christian faith is life lived in relationship to God.

Formed in the Anglican tradition in light of the Liturgical and Ecumenical movements,[6] what is foremost in this account is understanding Christian faith as a saving memory that is the conversion of the human person in "being made right" with God. This life is variously spoken of as participating in the divine life, as *theosis*, as reconciliation and redemption, as union with God, as the kingdom of God, as the beatific vision, as eternal life. In all, this is life in God as imaged in cross and resurrection that begins in creation, in losing oneself in the love of God and love of neighbor.

As a moral liturgical theology, chapter 1 begins with an account of the nature of conscience as addressed by Jesus and Socrates. This is to ask the question, "How do we come to know what to do?" Conscience is not the first and last of all knowledge of moral rules and principles, but a matter of moral consciousness, of how persons are attuned to the moral claims that form their lives. Conscience is a matter of memory, of how memory is formed and reformed in forming what we see and hear, in what we imagine, and how we respond in the life of the world.

Chapter 2, "The Scaffolding of Memory," offers an account of the development of human memory as the source of conscience. As described in neuropsychology, human development, and the process of language acquisition, the act of moral decision making is given in the movement from the memories of the past to anticipation and hopes for the future. This is not a deductive but an inductive process. Conscience is given in the embodied memory of lived experience as that memory is formed in language. As embodied memory, conscience is the memory of powers and purposes that make claims upon a person in the present to respond.

Chapter 3, "Word: The Memory of God," is an account of how the polyphony of voices that form Christian memory is a shared memory that attunes persons to a shared sense of the powers and purposes, constraints and connections, challenges and hopes that constitute the memory of God as what gives life. To make sense of Christian faith is to describe how this is so.

Moving from the polyphony of voices forming the Christian memory of God, chapter 4, "Sacrament: Incarnate Memory," turns to Christian communities as communities of worship. In worship, life in Christ is celebrated most centrally in the Eucharist. In the Eucharist, what is expressed in word is expressed in act, in the gathering of the community, in recognition and welcome, in song and prayer together, in hearing each other's voices in their particularity, in coming together around a table, in sharing bread and wine in remembrance of Jesus' life and teaching, death and resurrection, and in going out to live the life celebrated in the Eucharist, individually and corporately. At the center of the memory and call of God is the prophetic judgment breaking open the idols that tie Christian believing to the memories that narrowly turn attention to oneself.

Chapter 5, "Assembly: Many in One," focuses on the assembly as the Christian community of faith living out the memory of God in act. Central to this life are the practices that form the Christian memory of God in Christ as one's own and as shared together as one people; as the people of God. These practices are formed in dialogue with others and involve the examination and questioning of the memory of God in the life of the world and in one's own life. These are practices of worship, as well as what are called spiritual practices. For Christians these are Jewish practices that are further developed in light of schooling in the Hellenistic schools that develop from Plato's academy. Together they form the memory of God in Christ as a prophetic consciousness that breaks open the idols of the heart and turns attention in compassion to life together with others.

Chapter 6, "Church: One in Many," turns to the challenge of forming Christian communities together in one church in recognition of the faith they share in the memory and call of God given in the voices of many. This is the challenge of establishing an order of worship, of reading of scripture, and of teaching and discipline shared by the many such that the memory of God is not given in a singular narrative of God acting in history calling for their faith and fidelity in a promised future of personal fulfillment. This is the challenge of establishing an order where in each community piety is wedded to the prophetic memory and voice of God that is their own and that calls them into life together as one in many and many in one.

Chapter 7, "Hallowed Be Thy Name," concludes with reflections on the Lord's Prayer as the summary of the gospel to be prayed each day, as acclamation and invocation in drawing together the memory of God and in response calling for faith and fidelity in life together in the life of the world.

Introduction   xvii

SOURCES AND NOTES

In addition to referencing sources for each chapter, the chapter endnotes seek to serve readers seeking to follow and enter the interdisciplinary conversations that inform this book. A chronology at the end of the book identifies writings and events that may provide an historical context forming the memory of God in Christ. The chronology begins with Socrates and Plato in ancient Greece in the fifth century BCE and goes through the fourth century CE and the beginnings of Christendom in the establishment of Christianity as the religion of the Roman Empire. Bibliography, index of biblical texts, and index of names and subjects follow. Biblical quotations are from the New Revised Standard Version (NRSV) unless otherwise noted.

NOTES

1. Gordon Lathrop, *Saving Images: The Presence of the Bible in Christian Liturgy* (Minneapolis, MN: Fortress Press, 2017). In this book Lathrop offers an account of his liturgical theology and the grace of God given in the polyphony of the Bible that reveals what gives life as celebrated in the Eucharist and in the life of the assembly, grounded in the recognition and care of one another and especially in the stranger and those in need.

2. See Paul Ricoeur, "Nabert on Act and Sign," *The Conflict of Interpretations: Essays in Hermeneutics*," ed. Don Ihde (Evanston, IL: Northwestern University Press, 1974), 211–35. On Jean Nabert, see Nabert, *Elements for an Ethic*, tr. Paul Ricoeur and William J. Petrek (Evanston, IL: Northwestern University Press, 1969). For an introduction to Alfred Schutz, see Michael Barber, "Alfred Schutz," *The Stanford Encyclopedia of Philosophy* (Spring 2014 Edition). http://plato.stanford.edu/archives/spr2014/entries/schutz/. On Ricoeur, see John Wall, Moral Creativity: Paul Ricoeur and the Poetics of Possibility (New York: Oxford University Press, 2005). On Heidegger, see Judith Wolfe, *Heidegger and Theology* (New York: Bloomsbury, 2014).

3. Robert N. Bellah, *Religion in Human Evolution* (Cambridge, MA: Belknap Press of Harvard University Press, 2011); Charles Taylor, *A Secular Age* (Cambridge, MA: Belknap Press of Harvard University Press, 2007) and Taylor, *Sources of the Self: The Making of the Modern Identity* (Cambridge, MA: Harvard University Press, 1989).

4. H. Richard Niebuhr, *The Responsible Self: An Essay in Christian Moral Philosophy* (New York: Harper & Row, 1963), 42–46.

5. On the self in time and memory, see Niebuhr, *The Responsible Self,* 90–107. Also see Niebuhr's earlier account in *The Meaning of Revelation* (New York: Macmillan, 1941), esp. 91–137.

6. On the expression and development of Anglican understandings of Christian faith in its integral relationship to the liturgical renewal movement and the Ecumenical

Movement, see Sedgwick, "The Trajectory of Christian Mission," *Church, Society and the Christian Common Good: Essays in Conversation with Philip Turner*, ed. Ephraim Radner (Eugene, OR: Cascade Books, 2017), 34–42.

Chapter One

The Voice of God

In the story of the Good Samaritan (Lk. 10:25–37), a Samaritan sees a stranger in the ditch on the side of the road, beaten, helpless, lying between life and death. His heart is broken open. The Samaritan is moved in his belly—translated from the Greek word *splagchnon,* literally meaning moved in his "entrails." As though hearing a voice, the Samaritan is called to recognize the beaten man and respond. The response isn't calculated but immediate. It is natural. It reflects the fundamental openness of human persons to recognize and connect one to another.

Charles Taylor concludes his magisterial study of Christianity with this reading of the parable of the good Samaritan offered by Ivan Illich.[1] The Samaritan's response stands apart from the domestication of relations in roles and relations that form and preserve a social order for members of society. For Taylor, the recognition and embrace of the stranger is the source of radical conversion from the taken-for-granted roles and relations that distance person from the stranger and those in need. As a parable, the response of the Good Samaritan shocks those who have ears to hear into full-hearted awareness of what calls and claims them in the midst of life.

Likewise, the parable of the Prodigal Son (Lk. 15:11–31) is not a moral tale about a son who takes his inheritance and goes off in riotous living, spends his wealth, and finds himself bereft, feeding the pigs and having only what is left to feed himself. His repentance and return to his father's house, where he is forgiven, is not a reminder of the consequence of squandering what is given in riotous living. Instead, the parable shocks the reader in the telling of the father's response. The father sees his son on the horizon. Losing all composure, he runs to embrace and kiss his son who was lost and now is found, who was dead and is now alive. And the feast begins.

An earlier version of this chapter was first published as "Conscience and the Voice of God," *Sewanee Theological Review* 62 (Pentecost 2019) 3: 459–77.

CALLING INTO LIFE

A parable is a parable not because it teaches what is known but because it shocks the reader into recognition of what is hidden or forgotten.² "The kingdom of God is like a mustard seed. It is the smallest of all the seeds, but when it has grown, it is the greatest of shrubs and becomes a tree, so that all the birds of the air come and make nests in its branches" (Matt. 13:31–32). The mustard seed actually grows to be a scrawny bush, a far cry from the tall cedars of Lebanon that were used to build the ancient cities of Assyria and rebuild the temple in Jerusalem after the Jewish people returned from exile as conquered captives in Babylonia. Where the birds of the air find rest is not what you thought. The kingdom of God is not what you assumed. Life is not given in the power and riches that secure life from the threat of violence and decay. Life is given in daily life, in times of peace and times of violence. The voice of God is heard by those who hear the call to recognize and respond to family and friend, poor and rich, alone and rejected, blind and sick, dying and bereaved.

For Christians, the voice of God is remembered and heard again as spoken in scripture, in worship, and in the voices of the peoples of the world. The voice of God calling for recognition and response is imaged as calling for life lived in the love of God as the love of neighbor. The voice of God is imaged in the claim that "God is love" (1 Jn. 4:8, 16). Together, the images of life in God and God as love draw together stories and other images. In Paul's First Letter to the Corinthians, for example, love is imaged in terms of what love seeks: "Love is patient and kind . . . bears all things . . . [and] never ends" (1 Cor. 13:4–8). Love is to respond to others in need. As Jesus is remembered as saying in the Gospel of John after being asked by John the disciple whether he loves him, "Then feed my sheep." (Jn. 21: 15, 16, 17).

For some, love is a matter of the neighbor at hand. For others, love is seeking out those in need or is addressing matters of justice in society to ensure basic needs are met so that the poor and needy are no longer in need. Different claims need not be mutually exclusive. Different claims of love reflect what may be done in a particular time and place in life, in family, community, and society, and as a matter of time in life, in different roles and relations, reflecting different customs, cultures, and societies.

Love is not a moral idea that draws together a singular set of moral prescriptions that may be detailed in a universal moral law indicating what should be done. Rather, the image of love as the memory of God draws together different memories of the powers and purposes that call persons into life. The Christian memory of God is given in a polyphony of voices: in memories of Jesus' life, teaching, death, and resurrection; in the voices of

Hebrew scripture; in worship together in prayer and song; in rituals of celebration; in the lives of the gathered community; and in the voices remembered in one's own life and the life of the world. As judgment, invitation, and promise, the memory of God is a moral consciousness given in a polyphony of voices.[3] This is, as it were, the dispossession of ourselves in new life in the conversion and transformation of the oneself in time and memory. As Jesus is remembered teaching, "Those who try to make their life secure will lose it, but those who lose their life will keep it" (Lk. 17:33).[4]

MORAL CONSCIOUSNESS

The Christian memory of Jesus raised moral consciousness on one side of the Mediterranean as the voice of God calling persons into new life beyond what they knew. On the other side of the Mediterranean, Socrates, as remembered by Plato, questions what is known in seeking to know what to do.[5]

In Plato's writing there is no separate word for moral consciousness or what comes to be called "conscience." However, what is understood to be central to moral consciousness is what Socrates says in his response to the officials of Athens who accuse him of corrupting the youth and inciting them against those in authority. In his defense in the *Apology,* Socrates says, "I only ask questions about what is meant in saying something is beautiful and good. I only ask questions in knowing with myself that I know that I don't know."[6]

"Knowing with myself that I don't know" is, in Greek, the reflexive phrase, *synoida emauto.* This becomes objectified in the Greek word *syneidesis,* which is translated in Latin as *conscientia,* in French *concience,* and in English "conscience."[7] Before judgment about what to do, conscience must first refer to moral consciousness as beginning in knowing that I don't know.

The knowledge of knowing myself is that I know I am not wise at all, says Socrates. "Only God is wise."[8] This voice questions all that I know. It absolutely disorients the self, leaves the self in doubt, alone, naked, rejected, and exiled from the community that requires uncritical acceptance of its norms and customs. One is humiliated; humbled. In this disorientation, the human person is freed to question, to listen, to hear another, and to respond beyond the politics of interest and expediency. This knowing is a questioning and exploration of what it means to value something, such as the good, justice, honor, and virtue. This knowing begins with the experience of something that makes a claim upon us, but what exactly that is and what that requires is a continuing questioning, lest opinion be substituted for what is to be valued.

As in Plato's myth of the cave in *The Republic,*[9] what we see and believe is like living in a cave where we can only see shadows cast by the light. We are drawn to the light, but we cannot see the light outside the cave. The light is too bright, pure, blinding, beyond our sight. Lest we confuse the shadows from the light with the truth, the experience of doubt is fundamental to knowing. To doubt and know that we don't know is not skepticism or cynicism. To doubt and question is ground clearing. In doubt and questioning, a person becomes attuned to hear what is happening in the present beyond what is taken for granted and often required by law. In conversation, to question is to turn attention to another and hear and imagine what they suffer and what claims they make that likewise call us to respect and honor.

To follow the rule of law may be central to social life; however, political decisions necessarily reflect a "limited and partial perspective, measuring action and responsibility according to given norms and values."[10] Doubt and questioning, claims Socrates, is what a lover of wisdom (a philosopher) does. Nothing could be more important for the life of a people. And so, Socrates refuses to stop entering into conversations with the youth. Socrates speaks of his vocation as a response to a divine power acting upon him. He knows that life and his life are given in community such that he cannot plead guilty and disavow his vocation. When pressed by those in authority, he would rather die than accept exile. "I shall obey God rather than you."[11]

CARE AND ATTUNEMENT

Moral consciousness or conscience is not, first of all, a matter of what we know, of measuring and placing a value on what we see, and a judgment about what we should do. Moral consciousness is, first of all (to speak metaphorically), a voice beyond ourselves calling for recognition and care.

As the parables of the Good Samaritan and the Prodigal Son reveal, recognition of those who suffer begins in "the gut." The good Samaritan and the father of the prodigal son respond with compassion and care. The word "compassion" etymologically means "they suffer with the other" (from the Latin verb *pasi* meaning to suffer and *com* meaning with). Care is born of compassion. As described by Martin Heidegger in *Being and Time*, in German the word for care is *sorge*, which is translated in English as sorrow, care, and concern. Or we may say, compassion, care, and concern are together the fundamental mode of consciousness in being-in-the-world.[12]

What is original in human consciousness is a matter of attunement to the world. Heidegger makes this point vividly in the German word "dasein, literally translated in English as "being there." Attunement is a matter of how we are "being-there" in the world. What is original in human consciousness is reverence and care.[13]

To care is consciousness of being in the world, of being in time. To care might be to marvel in reverence at the turtle at rest or to be saddened at the wilting of the flowers. You might pick up the turtle and carry it to the other side of the road or you might water the flowers. Or you might seek to preserve the wetland by removing the invading trees. And then again, you might do none of these things. You might let nature take its course. But what stands before such decisions is a consciousness attuned to the goods that are not of our own making. As Erazim Kohák claims, whether the human person, the birds that fly, the forest dwellers, the denizens of the deep: all that lives between the water and the heavens and all that is given between the embers and the stars calls humans to a consciousness that is original in attuning human persons to the mystery of being.[14]

The word "attunement" is an apt description of moral consciousness as distinct from moral judgment.[15] Attunement conveys that moral consciousness is given before reflection and judgment. What we know is not something of our own making. What we see, hear, touch, smell, and taste acts upon us and focuses our attention. We stand in wonder about the beauty of the world about us.

Heidegger highlighted this attunement to the mystery of being in contrasting it to practical or pragmatic modes of consciousness.[16] In practical consciousness we seek to care for what we value in order to achieve some end, to realize some purpose. We see and judge things as sources to meet other needs, not least to meet human needs and desires, to realize human goals. The focus of practical consciousness is instrumental: to build a better shelter, to increase the harvest, to make clothing to wear, to establish an order that provides time to rest, to develop the knowledge and technology to create a new world of science and industry.

A SECULAR AGE

In his account of the secularism of the modern world, Charles Taylor develops the contrast between wonder and mastery, between a world of enchantment and a world governed by a pragmatic instrumentalism. Spoken of as "enlightenment," secularization is a rationalization of the world about us. The world is seen instrumentally in terms of cause and effect, as means to ends. Once understood, everything from the atomic building blocks of life to electromagnetic fields that power the world can be used to develop technologies to control the powers of nature, shape the world, and produce evermore human goods and services. As the world is commodified, human persons become narrowly attuned to the world. Human fulfillment is then conceived in terms of what is or can be accomplished.[17]

Of course, as Taylor describes, contrasts are misleading if they are read as either/or binary accounts of what is. Practical needs and interests are part of human life. The cold wind blows. In the flash of a moment, memory is activated in a practical manner. Given past ways of sheltering, the world is surveyed for newfound, possible forms of shelter. Possible actions are weighed in terms of practicality, time, effort, and so forth until a judgment is made and human action begins.

Still, while the world may become predominately perceived instrumentally, the world continues to awaken consciousness and attention to what acts upon us apart or beyond what is of practical use—the miracle of birth, the exuberance of play, the sound of music, the beauty of the wild, the coming of spring. As originary, moral consciousness is an awareness of and attention to "the rapture of the particular."[18]

Given the indubitable experience of moral consciousness as originary, God is the name that Christians (and others) have given to that which breaks in upon human awareness in the present and calls persons to care. This is the God of creation that is revealed in time in the face of what is other, in the human face, and in the face of nature. This is what is meant by speaking of God incarnate. Kohák says this simply: "God is—that is the all-pervasive clue, an awareness which precedes and underlies all subsequent inquiry, and which emerges in the guise of a conclusion at its end once humans rediscover the moral sense of nature."[19] To speak anthropomorphically in the theistic language of Judaism and Christianity, God calls upon humans to be recognized, to be acknowledged as God, as God who is Lord over all, almighty God, creator, sustainer, redeemer. This is the god that Christians come to address as Father, Son, and Holy Spirit.

Such acclamations attest to and attune persons to what is at hand breaking in upon them in time as sovereign, as giver of life beyond human control, as calling persons to respond into the newness of life, already and not yet. What we see now is shaped by what we have seen before. What we hear now is shaped by what we have heard before. Moral consciousness as hearing the voice of God calling us to respond now in reverence and care in this time and place is an apt expression of Christian faith and life.

TOWARDS THE MEMORY OF GOD

Given the competing claims of others, Socrates and Plato questioned those who claimed to know what made sense and what should be done. They called others into conversation to question and listen to others, to hear what formed a people in life together, and what formed people where corruption would destroy such a life. Jesus likewise was remembered in his life with others, in his teaching and in his dying, questioning and inviting others into a new way of life together. Those who followed in Christian communities of worship followed in conversations, questioning and hearing the voices of others, and in examining themselves in light of what is claimed calling for response.

Those who followed Socrates, Plato, and Jesus continued to ask the questions: How are memories formed and reformed? How are questions asked? How are claims and questions examined? What is the life into which persons are called? And how is that life to be passed on from one to another, from one generation to another? These are the questions central to forming schools of learning and the politics of life together. This is the focus of Plato's longest work, *The Republic*, and central to his forming the first school of teaching and formation in Athens, simply called "The Academy." Likewise, for Christians, these are the questions they addressed in forming Christian communities as one in faith shared together among communities of faith and their members who also differ in their expressions of faith and in particular judgments about what should and should not be done.

As this first chapter has sought to express, the argument of the book is twofold. First, in response to the historicity of human life and meaning, Christian faith and moral consciousness are understood in terms of the nature of human memory. As attunement to what is of value that calls for attention and response, human consciousness is a moral consciousness. Second, the memory of God is formed together in Christian communities as communities of worship. Together, this book offers what may be called a moral liturgical theology.

NOTES

1. Ivan Illich, *The Rivers North of the Future, The Testament of Ivan Illich as told to David Cayley*, ed. David Cayley (Toronto, Canada: House of Anansi Press, 2005), 207–8, 222–23; quoted in Charles Taylor, *A Secular Age* (Cambridge, MA: Belknap Press of Harvard University Press, 2007), 158, 737–744.2.

2. See John Dominic Crossan, *In Parables* (New York: Harper & Row, 1973); *The Dark Interval* (Niles, IL: Argus, 1975); and *Raid on the Articulate* (New York: Harper & Row, 1976); On the hermeneutical turn in literary criticism and biblical scholarship from the meaning behind the text to reader-response theory and what has become reception criticism in biblical and historical scholarship, see Norman Perrin, *Gospel and Parables* (Minneapolis, MN: AugsburgFortress, 2003).

3. On the memory of Jesus as a polyphony of memories in forming a Christian ethic, see Allen Verhey, *Remembering Jesus: Christian Community, Scripture, and the Moral Life* (Grand Rapids, MI: Eerdmans, 2002).

4. See parallels Mk. 8:35, Matt. 10:39; Jn. 12:25.

5. See Mika Ojakangas, *The Voice of Conscience: A Political Genealogy of Western Ethics Experience* (New York: Bloomsbury, 2013), 221. The argument here follows that of Ojakangas, 213–24.

6. Plato, *Apology, The Dialogues of Plato,* tr. Benjamin Jowett (New York: Random House, 1937.), 21b; Ojakangas, 215–17.

7. *Oxford English Dictionary,* "conscience," online entry.

8. Plato, *Apology,* 23a.

9. Plato, *The Republic*,14a–520a; Ojakangas, 222.

10. See Illich, 186–93.

11. Plato, *Apology,* 29b; see Ojakanagas, 218–24.

12. Martin Heidegger, "Letter on Humanism," Basic Writings, ed. David Farrell Krell (New York: HarperPerennial, 2008), 213–65; and in *Being and Time,* tr. John Macquarrie and Edward Robinson (New York: Harper & Row, 1962), Division One, VI: 196–269, with his account of care as the being of dasein, and Division Two, II: 231–341, with his account of conscience, being-whole, and being-toward death. For an introduction to Heidegger, see Michael Wheeler, "Martin Heidegger, *The Stanford Encyclopedia of Philosophy*, ed. Edward N. Zalta (Winter 2018 Edition), 2.2.7, https://plato.stanford.edu/ archives/win2018/entries/heidegger/.

13. Most notable in seeing reverence as the ground of moral consciousness was Albert Schweitzer, *Reverence for Life,* tr. Reginald H. Fuller (New York: Harper & Row, 1969). See also Paul Woodruff, *Reverence: Renewing a Forgotten Virtue* (New York: Oxford University Press, 2001).

14. Erazim Kohák, *The Embers and the Stars: A Philosophical Inquiry into the Moral Sense of Nature* (Chicago: The University of Chicago Press, 1984).

15. Attunement is a translation of "stimmung" *in* Heidegger's *Being and Time.* On Heidegger and Stimmung, see John Haugeland, *Dasein Disclosed: John Haugeland's Heidegger,* ed. Joseph Rouse (Cambridge, MA: Harvard University Press, 2013), 144–46.

16. See Heidegger, "Letter on Humanism," *Martin Heidegger: Basic Writings*, ed. David Farrell Krell, tr. Frank A. Capuzzi (London: HarperPerennial, 2008), 217–19, 258.

17. Heidegger, *Ibid.* Charles Taylor, "Disenchantment-Reenchantment," *Dilemmas and Connections: Selected Essays* (Cambridge, MA: The Belknap Press of Harvard University Press, 2011), 287–302.

18. To paraphrase Charles Altieri title in his exposition of an aesthetics of affects. See *The Particulars of Rapture: An Aesthetics of Affects* (Ithaca, NY: Cornell University Press, 2003).

19. Kohák, 196.

Chapter Two

The Scaffolding of Memory

Understandings of memory have been developed by scholars working in developmental psychology, neuroscience, evolutionary biology, and cultural anthropology, as well as linguistically and philosophically in terms of signification. Together, these studies describe what may be imaged as "the scaffolding of memory." Their work makes clear that memory is the memory of the body that in word and act is remembered as shared with others in forming life together. The metaphor of scaffolding reflects how memories are formed from the bottom up, from life lived to life imaged and shared to attuning persons to the life of the world and in response forming new memories of what gives life.[1]

EMBODIED MEMORY

I want to begin an account of the nature of memory with the work of Daniel N. Stern. Trained as a clinician and researcher, Stern dedicated his work to an empirically based understanding of human development through the observations of the interactions between mother and child. His work is most fully developed in *The Interpersonal World of the Infant*, which was given a more popular, narrative exposition in *Diary of a Baby: What Your Child Sees, Feels, and Experiences.*[2] A discussion of the game of peek-a-boo offers a concrete description of the nature of human memory as it develops from human consciousness of the world.

In its simplest terms, the development of human memory is evidenced in the game of peek-a-boo in which mother and child look into each other's eyes, turn away, and return to gaze again with delight. Mother looks the baby in the eye and the child responds by acknowledging that look. Eyes open, eyebrows raise, a smile, a sound of the voice. The mother responds with a smile and sound of glee and then covers her face. The baby turns away, and then the mother reappears from another place saying, "Here's mommy," and again looks into the baby's eyes. The baby's eyes widen. She smiles again. Her body shivers in what is interpreted as delight. The mother turns away again, and the play continues.

As Stern has done in *Diary of a Baby,* to express the recognition of another and in that the fact of human memory, the voice of the infant playing peek-a-boo may be imagined (though, of course, that is impossible as the infant is prelinguistic). In telling an imaginary story of peek-a-boo, the infant might think, I see her and smile. She smiles. She is gone. I look for her. She appears, smiles, and says, "Here's Mommy." I catch her eyes and gaze into them and smile back with a sound of glee, and she's gone again. I know she has gone but wait expectantly until she reappears. I know Mommy is here and gone and will be back again. My smile and glee express and signify to her my pleasure in her being there. So, in turn, her eyes, voice, and smile express and tell me she is pleased to being together, in touch.

In peek-a-boo is the tale of memory. Peek-a-boo is an improvisational series of gestures and responses. The fact of memory is evidenced in the infant's anticipation that "mother" will return; in remembering they connect to each other. They feel the presence of another who recognizes them and who feels recognized by them. In memory, they are connected and attuned to the world in expectation.

The game of peek-a-boo also evidences how language develops as a word or sign (like the word "Mommy") is remembered and brings to memory what has been experienced as something—such as an object of perception, a series of events, or some relationship between objects and events. In this way, language is the extension or expansion of memory.[3] The word "Mommy" begins for the infant with the pairing of "Here's Mommy" with the unified action of the one who gestures, responds, and recognizes. Other actions and meanings may then be paired with this person. She is the one who feeds, comforts, watches, walks, plays, reads, turns away, and returns. Such actions over time are remembered as a pattern of responses that are later signified and remembered in names such as "mothering" or "parenting," or in more complicated associations in names such as "good parenting" and "bad parenting."

As words are paired together, the sense of the world is enlarged in what is perceived and known. Further, following the gaze of each other, parent and child share the experience of each other and the world they share together. Together they may look at an object or follow a series of perceptions as an object crosses their shared horizon of sight. Someone may speak a word that gives a name to the object of attention: tree, sky, bird, fly, evening, night, moon, stars. Or someone else may point to an object that moves across the horizon of sight and utter a phrase: "goodbye," or "good night, moon." Words paired with objects and events are repeated and remembered until words bring to consciousness the objects and events to which they are paired.

Words are also paired with other words, drawing attention to relationships that may extend to the larger world. These may be expressed conceptually, mathematically, or otherwise. Words give voice to what are together perceived as the same and different kinds of objects and relations, of plants and animals, trees and birds, seasons of the year, sanity and madness, beauty and goodness, powers and purposes, the temporal and the eternal. The scaffolding of language forms the power of language that forms the human memory of God.

WORD AND THE VISION OF GOD

This process of language acquisition is most clearly evidenced in the life of Helen Keller.[4] Struck by an early childhood illness before the age of two, Helen Keller lost her sight and hearing and was left with the primary sense of touch. While she subsequently was able to make hand signals to communicate with her childhood companion and family members, in the summer of 1887, just before her seventh birthday, Anne Sullivan joined the Keller family to work with Helen in learning to communicate. Sullivan began by having Keller touch an object and then by writing in the palm of Keller's hands the letters of the word. Beginning with the doll she had brought as a gift, Sullivan inscribed the letters d-o-l-l. With repetition, Keller imitated the inscription. The move from imitation to signification came promptly, and Keller spent the day learning words.

As Keller recounts in her autobiography, the power of words was more than naming objects of experience. Words had the power to extend her sense of things, to feel deep connections that formed the world in which she lived. This was dramatically expressed in learning the word "water." When Sullivan paired the inscription w-a-t-e-r with the running water over her hand, Keller writes, "I stood still, my whole attention fixed upon the motions of her fingers. Suddenly I felt a misty consciousness as of something forgotten—a thrill of returning thought; and somehow the mystery of language was revealed to me. I knew then that w-a-t-e-r meant the wonderful cool something that was flowing over my hand." That day, she goes on to say, the words she learned did more than name objects and persons. Words brought to consciousness more than what they signified. They brought an awareness that was a feeling "of kinship with the rest of the world."[5]

Soon Keller moved from objects and persons to events and relations. "Think" was her first such word. It became a word to her when she was having difficulty in choosing beads of different sizes in order to string them in a series of repeating, symmetrical order. Anne Sullivan pointed to her forehead and inscribed t-h-i-n-k. Keller knew that this inscribed word was the process or event going on in her head and that she should focus and "think." This was her first time where a word referred to more than an object or event. The word "think" referred to the head or brain. But more than the head, the word "think" referred to thinking, to concentrating in order to figure something out.

Remembering when Sullivan wrote in her hand, "I love Helen," Keller now asked, "What is love?" She knew love was not a thing but something more. The word referred to some larger meaning between Anne Sullivan and herself. In the following conversation, as Keller described it, Sullivan offered several analogies, affirmations, and negations.

> Love is something like the clouds that were in the sky before the sun came out. You cannot touch the clouds, you know; but you feel the rain and know how glad the flowers and the thirsty earth are to have it after a hot day. You cannot touch love either; but you feel the sweetness that it pours into everything. Without love you would not be happy or want to play.

In reflecting on her thoughts, Keller continues, "The beautiful truth burst upon my mind. I felt that there were invisible lines stretched between my spirit and the spirits of others."[6]

As distinct from a name, we might say, the idea of love was born for Helen Keller in her body. The word "loved" was paired with her affective response to a set of relations she had remembered and as signified and effected by the words Anne Sullivan connected to the word "love." We could say, the word "love" signified and effected—it re-presented affectively—the events and relations that are signified and felt by the word "love" as paired in memories of the body.

From these beginnings, the life of Helen Keller developed as language unfolded with the life she shared with others. Her world expanded further as she learned to speak as she approached her tenth birthday. Having had the beginnings of speech before losing hearing and sight, Keller learned to give voice to the letters of the alphabet and then to words themselves. Learning to speak followed intensive work with Sarah Fuller, the principal of the Horace Mann School for the Deaf in Boston and continued with Anne Sullivan. Feeling the position of tongue and lips, the vibrations of the throat and the movements of the mouth, she imitated Fuller and Sullivan who then offered feedback. With, as she writes, "Practice, practice, practice," until she could feel "the proper ring in her voice," Keller repeated "words or sentences, sometimes for hours."[7] With speech, conversations enlarged the richness of language, her understandings of others, and the development of a critical perspective on the world.

The rest is history. Mainstreamed in "school learning," Keller read voraciously and completed a demanding curriculum in literature, history, mathematics, science, and foreign languages (elementary Greek, advanced

Latin, French, and German). She was accepted and graduated from Radcliffe College in 1904 as an elected member of Phi Beta Kappa. Blind and deaf, she became a member of the Socialist Party, and until her death in 1968, was an advocate for the marginalized through political advocacy, public speaking, writing, and supporting and raising funds for a range of organizations. All this was a consequence of her moral consciousness, which was formed through the distinctive human capacity for language. From image to story, language gave her the power to see, to make sense of life, and to speak for those who had no voice.

As reflected in the studies of childhood development and in Helen Keller's life, the movement from gesture to response to mutual recognition of one another and to a shared world develops through the human capacity for memory and language. Developed through shared attention, language names and extends awareness of objects, relations, and events that form the world to give names to relationships and broader powers and purposes.[8]

THE SCIENCE OF THE MIND

What accounts of human development describe the science of mind confirms. Living beings respond to constraints and possibilities through their capacity to remember. Studies in neurobiology and neuropsychology have begun to understand the bodily processes that correspond to the descriptive accounts of learning and language acquisition. While nerve cells (neurons) were first identified in the late nineteenth century, it was not, however, until the 1960s that Eric Kandel discovered the biochemical mechanism of neurons that form the neural circuitry that accounts for how memory and learning happen, for which he won the Nobel Prize in Medicine in 2000.[9]

Through specific experiments on sea slugs (*Aplysia*), Kandel described how the presentation of a stimulus affected neuron response and how when given repeatedly the biochemistry of the neurons changed. Repetition accounted for the difference between short and long-term memory. As reflected in the game of peek-a-boo, the look of the infant leads to the response of the mother, whose gaze into the eyes of the infant leads to the excitement of mutual recognition. As gesture and response are repeated, the infant remembers the sequence of gestures and responses. When eyes meet and the mother hides, the attention of the infant waits for the reappearance of the mother.

Kandel concludes his studies of the biochemical processes of learning and memory at the micro level of neuron circuitry with two questions. First, to use an anthropomorphic metaphor, how is the desire for the unity of human experience to be understood? Second, as something desired distinct from what is given, how is self-consciousness as the experience of the self-acting to create something new to be understood? Kandel sees these two questions as the focus of what is now called "the science of the mind."[10] At the heart of these two questions is understanding the development of language. From research in neurobiology and neuropsychology, two models of the self have developed.

Terrence Deacon describes these two models of the self as the "computational self" and the "mindful self."[11] The computational model focuses on causal nexuses to understand the biochemical processes that constitute memory. The model of the self as mindful focuses on the "teleodynamic processes" of organisms in order to understand how the self responds to the world in which it lives by forming capacities to act in new ways that thereby change the world. The science of mind provides understandings of language as reflecting and effecting the human desire for unity and the experience of self-consciousness as agency in the world.

THE COMPUTATIONAL SELF

In viewing the human self in computational terms, the mind is identified with the brain as the organ that functions like an organic computer processing data as information that leads to human action. Neuroscience describes the causal relationships between neural processes and human responses as analogous to a computer program. This includes describing biochemical processing of stimuli, for example, differences between sensory and motor neurons, changes in neurons that determine short- and long-term memory, and the mapping of neural processing within and between different parts of the brain.

As Eric Kandel describes his own research, how the neural processes work together in the use of language is illumined by how and why they sometimes fail to work. The diagnosis and treatment of neurological diseases and disorders through drug therapies or brain surgery have provided such understanding. These include treatment of strokes, tumors, epilepsy, multiple sclerosis, Parkinson's disease, schizophrenia, anxiety, depression, manic-depression, and attention deficit disorder.[12]

In the computational model, understanding the neurological process in the formation and use of language begins with understanding how the brain effects representation of past experience and representations of possible futures. The power of memory (like a computer algorithm) may from the variety of elements experienced in the past offer a framework or program that images and interprets the past and projects likely futures.

Moving from memory to mind requires the additional steps of making sense of the human experience of judgment and action, of being the agent of change. This entails making sense of self-consciousness as the experience of the self as agent and of how this experience expresses more than a strict causal process. In the model of the computational self, consciousness is the experience that accompanies the five senses (perception, hearing, feeling, tasting, and smelling). Consciousness is sentience, not as a separate entity or power but as the experience of neurological processes.

THE MINDFUL SELF

Understanding self-consciousness as a form of sentience, however, does not describe neurological processes that would make sense of self-reflection and the experience of human freedom and agency. Consciousness as sentience doesn't make sense of the Socratic claim that conscience begins with knowing that you don't know and, hence, are able to question what is remembered, identify the sources for the claims about what should be done, envision possible courses of action, assess what is to be honored or dismissed, weigh what may be gained or lost, and make a decision about what possible future will be sought in act.

Given the computational model, understanding moral consciousness becomes focused through magnetic resonance imaging (MRIs) on how different parts of the brain, working together, process neural information. Whether descriptions that focus on causal nexuses can make sense of what is meant by critical thought and what it means to speak of human freedom and agency in creating the future is questioned by those engaged in the science of the mind.[13]

Terrence Deacon claims that understanding human thought and action in terms of ends and purposes requires an additional, broader focus than the focus on causal nexuses. As the model of the self as mindful seeks to convey, human purposefulness is not something beyond nature, a power apart from the body, a soul conceived as a supernatural power separate from the body. Such dualism fails to understand the nature of memory and the process of formation that leads to human mindfulness as awareness of and responsiveness to what gives life. Such dualism leads to a metaphysical dualism that contradicts what is known about human action from the natural sciences. Instead, Deacon claims, mindfulness is to understand how human persons come to respond to their environment, to the world in which they live, as part of a whole. This relationship is teleological imaged as analogous to the paired relationship of figure and ground, organism and environment, self and other.

Deacon describes in detail what purposefulness means in teleodynamic terms. Organisms do not change simply by means of the random chance of stimulus and response. Rather, organisms adapt to changes in the environment in which they live by developing new capabilities that, in turn, change the environment. Together these changes create both new possibilities and constraints that form the continuing response and development of the organism and of the ecosystem of which it is a part.

As Deacon says, "Adaptive features can be understood as adaptive only because of their contribution to something else, a larger system that they happen to be a part of."[14] Quoting Immanuel Kant as offering "probably the most prescient and abstract characterization of the dynamic logic of organism design," he writes, "an organized being is . . . not a mere machine, for that has merely *motive power*, but it possesses in itself *formative power* of a self-propagating kind which it communicates to its materials though they have it not of themselves."[15]

The distinctive (if possibly not entirely unique) formative power for humans is language. The difference between those who have language and those who don't is so radical that it would be appropriate, writes Deacon, to speak of what is virtually a new species, *Homo symbolicus*.[16] Language gives humans the power to interpret the world, to remember the past, and to imagine possible futures and thereby in act to adapt to constraints and possibilities in forming themselves and the world together. In this way, humans and the world together share in an emergent future of purposes and values that give life.

THE SCAFFOLDING OF MEMORY

The human development of language begins in remembering names and what they are paired with. From there language develops to express worlds of meaning that interpret the world in which humans live. The scaffolding of memory is given in language. At their simplest, words are signs that have a single reference. Generally, though, the name of a word—*light, dark, book, box, water, large, small*—is arbitrary (or at least any mimetic connection is long forgotten). In either case, a word is paired with something until the two are remembered together. Sometimes words have a double reference. For example, a word may be paired with another word that qualifies what is signified in the first word: a sunny day, warm water, a good cake, a small man. A word may also be paired with a series of actions—meal, reading, hospitality, friendship—and further paired with the words drawing together common memories of human actions: shared meal, difficult reading, extended hospitality, supportive friendship. So, the world is scaffolded from the particularity of lived experience to the pairing of images with lived experience (or we might say, with life lived) paired with other images paired with narrative renderings of life lived in the world in the broader and broadest sense of what makes sense, of what gives life.

From objects to powers and purposes to what it is to be, to what it is to be alive. the scaffolding of memory is symbolic as a word is paired with other memories expressed in words and stories that reach down to the memories lived experiences. The stop sign signifies a sign at the side of the road. It also signifies a command to stop and further brings to consciousness the memory of police officers and what they can do. Still further is the memory of what is meant by law as an order that is not simply a matter of power and authority but of purposes, variously expressed by other symbols such as justice, equality, and the common good.

Other names reference more abstract relations. Consider such names as the good, beauty, justice, and the word "God." In themselves, such names may be considered conceptual symbols. As conceptual, their breadth and unifying power are tied to a range of more particular images and stories that draw together, each in their own particular way, the lived experience of others. The power of conceptual symbols such as justice, good, evil, and the beautiful reveal and bring to memory the sense of what is valued and calls for recognition and response in the particularities of life lived beyond a singular memory given at a particular time and place. For example, the image "ecology" expresses the integral relationships that form an environment in such a way that a part can't be understood apart from the whole. The word "ecology" is symbolic as it brings to consciousness the sense of the world as fundamentally connected, where life is interdependent, where life is given together. The word "ecology" is given in the memory of a range of images, stories, and understandings of the life of the world remembered anew, together as integrally related and interdependent, even as in life they may also be juxtaposed or even in conflict: rivers, wetlands, meadow and mountains, forest, flora, fauna, insects, birds, fish, and mammals, sun and rain, seasons of the year.

This pairing of "lived experience" with images that remember those experiences, paired with other images that express a broader sense of the world forms the "scaffold of memory." For example, for Helen Keller, the experience of water flowing into her hand pairs together lived experience with the image of water with the image flowing. The words "flowing water" signify and bring to awareness the lived experiences of water flowing and the lived experience of life itself. The river of life that flows through us all is remembered as the experience of life, of play, of friendships, of the lives of the world in the seasons of the year, in living and dying.[17]

In language, humans have the capacity to name, to signify what they experience in time and over time. In language is consciousness of what is beyond the moment. Words not only bring to consciousness the memory of specific experiences. Humans are able to remember different memories of what they have experienced in the past. In such remembering, humans are self-conscious. They are conscious of how they have changed. From these memories they are able to express what they experience in such words as constraints and connections, challenges and possibilities, fears and sadness, joy and gladness, cares and concerns. Together, in the scaffolding of memory, humans can image what has happened to them and what they have suffered, as the experience of powers that have acted upon them. And they can name those actions in terms of their experience of being in time.

In language is the power to give expression to things beyond the singularities of memory imprinted in the body. Language is the alchemical power to figure and transfigure, to cast spells over one way of seeing to create other ways of seeing, to attune the self to being in the world.

NOTES

1. Central to this social development of memory as embodied is Alfred Schutz's phenomenology of the social world. As imaged as "the scaffolding of memory," Schutz moves from shared attention to human signs and symbols that form linguistic worlds of meaning that reflect and effect human memory and understandings. See Alfred Schutz, *The Phenomenology of the Social World* (Evanston, IL: Northwestern University Press, 1967), 97–138. Also see Schutz, "Symbol, Reality and Society," *Collected Papers* I, ed. Maurice Natanson (The Hague: Martinus Hijhoff, 1971), 287–305.

2. Daniel N. Stern, *The Interpersonal World of the Infant* (New York: Basic Books, 1985), with a twenty-nine-page introduction written in 2000 for a new edition that reviewed and updated his earlier work in light of developing research, including that done in neuroscience. For his more popular, imaginative narrative account of child development from the point of view of the child from birth to age four, see *Diary of a Baby* (New York: Basic Books, 1990).

3. In what follows in terms of memory and the pairing of signs (and symbols) to objects of consciousness (features and relationships) in time, see Schutz's account of what George Herbert Meade described in terms of the self and the generalized other in *Mind, Self, and Society* (Chicago: University of Chicago Press, 1934), See note 1 above and *Collected Papers II: Studies in Social Theory*, ed. Arvid Brodersen (The Hague: Martinus Nijhoff,1964), "Making Music Together," 159–78 and other essays in applied theory.

4. Helen Keller with Anne Sullivan, John A. Macy, *Story of My Life* (New York: Doubleday, 1903)

5. Keller, 12.

6. Keller, 14.

7. Keller, 25.

8. On Keller and the nature of language development as sign and symbol, see Merlin Donald, *A Mind So Rare: The Evolution of Human Consciousness* (New York: Norton, 2001), 235–51.

9. Eric R. Kandel, *In Search of Memory: The Emergence of a New Science of Mind* (New York: W.W. Norton, 2006), 142, 160. The book as a whole offers a fulsome account of the history of the development of neuroscience.

10. Kandel, 376–84.

11. Terrence W. Deacon, *Incomplete Nature: How Mind Emerged from Matter* (New York: W. W. Norton, 2013), 485–507. See Robert K. Logan, "The Terrance Deacon's Incomplete Nature: How Mind Emerged from Matter. A Review and Précis of *An Incomplete Nature*," *ETC: A Review of General Semantics* 71 (Oct. 2014) 4: 301–23; https://www.jstor.org/stable/24761945.

12. Kandel, 323–75.

13. Kandel, 382.

14. Deacon, *Incomplete Nature,* 123. See chapter 9, "Teleodynamics," 264–87. In defining teleodynamic, Deacon writes, "A form of dynamical organization exhibiting end-directedness and consequence-organized features that is constituted by the co-creation, complementary constraint, and reciprocal synergy of two or more strongly coupled morphodynamic processes" (552). See the early development of this argument by Stuart Kauffman, *At Home in the Universe. The Search for the Laws of Self-Organization and Complexity* (New York: Oxford University Press, 1995). For a contemporary example on the development of the ecosystem of forests, see Suzanne Sinard, *Finding the Mother Tree* (Alfred A. Knopf, 2021).

15. Deacon, *Incomplete Nature,* 302. Here as throughout, Deacon argues against the reification of processes as substances occupying time and space, as in speaking of body and soul, mind and body, the passions of the body, the power of consciousness, the place of memory, the freedom of the will, or the conscience of the soul. Instead, these names indicate teleodynamic processes that move towards equilibrium, those that move against or apart from equilibrium, and those that are intentionally directed (512). More broadly, see his discussion of the enduring philosophical discussion of this problem in terms of realism and nominalism (184–87) and revisioning nominalism and realism in understanding ends (teloi) as emerging in response to constraints (481–84).

16. Terrence W. Deacon, *The Symbolic Species: The Co-evolution of Language and the Brain* (New York: Norton, 1997), 341. In terms of evolutionary biology, see Merlin Donald, *Origins of the Modern Mind* (Cambridge, MA: Harvard University Press, 1991) and *A Mind So Rare: The Evolution of Human Consciousness* (New York: Norton, 2001). Also see Bellah, *Religion in Human Evolution* for an account of this literature, 131–33.

17. This is what is meant by the metaphorical character of language as symbolic. This is at the center of Paul Ricoeur's hermeneutical phenomenology as the human, creative response to being-in-time as voluntary and involuntary, self and other, fallen and redeemed. On metaphor see Paul Ricoeur, *The Rule of Metaphor,* tr. Robert Czerny (Toronto: University of Toronto Press, 1977). For the most comprehensive account of Ricoeur's poetics in understanding the moral self, see John Wall, *Moral Creativity: Paul Ricoeur and the Poetics of Possibility* (Oxford: Oxford University Press, 2005), on metaphor, 30–35.

Chapter Three

Word: The Memory of God

The memory of God is given or, we may say, is revealed in the language that gives voice to the powers of change that make sense of our lives. Whether addressing divine spirits in song led by aboriginal spiritual leaders and healers or praying in offering formalized prayers recited from memory or from a prayerbook, the language of divine powers and spirits, of gods and of God is learned and brings to consciousness the powers that create and form life from the beginning of time. These include creation accounts and stories about struggles with evil spirits, miracle healings, angelic encounters, and accounts of judgment now and at the end of time. In this way, words such as *creator* and *redeemer*, *holy* and *mighty*, *love* and j*ustice*, *life* and *death* draw together meanings from more particular renderings of life at a particular time and place.

Apart from the scaffolding of images from the bottom up, God is only a name (a transcendental signifier) that floats above experience as an empty sign. Disconnected from memories of events in time and place, the word "God" brings to consciousness nothing. Connected to the memories of being in time, the power of the language of God is in attuning the human person to what gives and what destroys life in the world beyond a moment in time, beyond a particular event or set of events. Such is the Christian memory of God grounded in the Jewish memory of God taken up anew in the memory of Christ.

THE PRAYER BOOK OF THE BIBLE

By the end of the fourth century CE, Hebrew scripture and the twenty-seven New Testament texts came to be accepted by Christian communities of worship as Christian scripture. These included the Book of Psalms. What was acclaimed as holy scripture was not a singular voice but many voices, sometimes in harmony together and sometimes juxtaposed and dissonant one to another. Together, divided as Old and New Testament, the books of the Bible are one book, a book of books that as prayed in 150 psalms expressed and formed the Christian memory of God as known in Christ.[1] Recalling Martin Luther and the use of the Book of Psalms in worship, Dietrich Bonhoeffer said simply, the psalms are "the prayer book of the Bible."[2]

Like the books of the Christian Bible, the Book of Psalms, together and not apart, formed the Christian memory of God.[3] Together the psalms form a polyphony of different memories of God that variously complement one another and are juxtaposed one to another, together informing, questioning, and reforming the memory of God and of life lived in relationship to God.

From the beginning of the first psalm in the book of psalms, the psalms are prayers that delight in the way of God as the way of life over and against the way of wickedness and death. Psalms give thanks and praise for all that is created in its glory and richness. Psalms give thanks for God's covenant with Abraham and in the promise of making Israel a great and prosperous nation. The psalms are songs seeking freedom from oppression in exile in Egypt, and they are cries for justice against those who oppress others for their own gain.

Psalms recall God's call for fidelity to the way of the Lord, tell of the failure of Israel to be faithful, and give voice to the prophets to call for repentance and return to the ways of justice for all, especially welcoming and caring for the stranger and those in need. Psalms recall the failure to heed the call of prophets, the fall of their kingdom, and their exile in Babylonia. Psalms are songs of lament, "woe is me," songs calling for retribution, and songs of a contrite heart beseeching God to come and save us. Psalms plead for comfort and for new life. And psalms pray that God may be merciful in judgment, remain faithful to the promise of the covenant, and restore the fortunes of Israel.

Following their liberation from exile in Babylonia by the Persians at the end of the sixth century BCE, the Jewish people returned to their ancestral lands centered in Jerusalem and began the building of the second Temple. Psalms of praise and thanks to God as God of history were taken up again. The Roman victory ending the Jewish rebellion seeking independence concluded in the destruction of the second temple in 70 CE. New memories were heard and remembered in the psalms, including that in suffering, God alone may be known beyond what has been. "For God alone my soul waits in silence; from him alone comes my salvation" (Ps. 62).

Again, the psalms bring together in memory the many voices of scripture, including antinarratives that directly question other voices. The story of Job questions the stories that God's order is about human fulfillment as humans see it, and so questions the nature of God. Job asks, "Shall we receive the good at the hand of God, and not receive the bad?" (Job 2:10). Together in harmony and juxtaposed in dissonance, the play of memories reveals the memory of God in time, not as self-fulfillment but as the memory, the revelation of what it is to be in time. In the psalms, the memory of God attunes persons to God as it addresses God in joy and gladness, sufferings and sorrows, anger, and hope.

In the play of voices, in juxtaposition and in questioning, the Jewish and Christian memory of God is iconoclastic. The power of language to become attuned to God is also the power to turn from the memory of God in the voice of many to the memory of God paired with a singular image in what is imagined as what would be the fulfillment of one's own life. The memory and faith in God as One in many carries with it the first basic prophetic call of God, expressed in the first two of the Ten Commandments given to Moses: "You shall have no other gods but me" and "You shall not make for yourself any idol" (Ex. 20:3,4; Deut. 5:7,8). This is the prophetic call of God as the word of judgment to those who seek to establish the world as their own and fail to hear the call of God in the voice of others calling for recognition and care in the name of the justice of God.

AN OLD SONG, A NEW SONG

For Christians, the psalms are an old song sung anew in the memory of love and hope revealed in Jesus in the life of the world and in the prophetic call of judgment and vision of new life breaking in and calling all into a new life together.

The memory of God in Christ is something old and something new in their lives. The earliest Christian hymns (called "canticles," from the Latin denoting small songs) are songs of the memory of Jesus as the Messiah. Included in the written text of the Gospel of Luke, three of these earliest canticles came to be sung as part of Christian daily worship: the *Magnificat* as the song of Mary (Lk. 1:46–55), the *Benedictus Dominus Deus* as the song of Zechariah (Lk. 1:68–79), and the *Nunc Dimittis* as the Song of Simeon (Lk. 2:29–32). In these early songs of the Church, the memory of Jesus is the song of God as the God of justice "who has scattered the proud in the imagination of their hearts . . . put down the mighty from their thrones . . . exalted the lowly . . . filled the hungry with good things . . . and the rich . . . sent away empty" (Lk. 1:51–53). This is God who "has raised up for us a mighty savior . . . that he would save us from our enemies . . . to shine on those who dwell in darkness and the shadow of death, and to guide our feet into the way of peace" (Lk. 1:69, 71, 79). And, in remembering the suffering servant in Isaiah (Is. 49:6), this is the savior who "has set your servant free to go in peace as you have promised . . . for all the world to see: to be a light to enlighten the nations" (Lk. 1:31, 33).[4]

In the many voices of scripture, the memory of God in Christ isn't plotted out in a singular narrative. Like the psalms and canticles, the play of different images and stories of God in Christ call those who hear to attention and into the life of God in the life of the world. As something old and something new, they hear the memory of God as the memory of the past that opens them to God as being in time. This is the truth that the prophet Isaiah proclaims at the time of the Babylonian conquest of Israel. "Remember not the former things, nor consider the things of old. Behold, I am doing a new thing; now it springs forth, do you not perceive it? I will make a way in the wilderness and rivers in the desert." (Is. 43:18–19)[5]

GOD INCARNATE

As early Christians gathered together to share a meal, to pray, and to share memories of Jesus, bread and wine came to be paired with memories of Jesus' last supper. As reflected in song, in canticles, the memory of the last meal with Jesus recalls the Israelites' last meal at the beginning of their exodus into a new life freed from slavery in Egypt. Bread and wine represent the basic foods of life; gifts of creation. Breaking bread together and sharing wine bring to memory what gives life in life together. Given the memory of Jesus' last supper with his disciples, where Jesus called upon them to "do this in remembrance of me," the memory of God in Christ came to be imaged in bread and wine. Jesus is remembered as saying, "This is my body which is broken for you . . . This cup is a new covenant in my blood" (1Cor 11:23–26; Matt 26:26–29; Mark 14:22–25; Lk. 22:15–20).

Shared together in gathering in prayer and worship, bread and wine are paired in memory with Jesus' crucifixion and death and with resurrection and new life. As that came to be remembered in the Gospel of John, following their meal together, Jesus gets up from the table and washes the feet of the disciples (Jn. 13:4–5) and says to them, "Peace I leave with you; my peace I give you" (Jn. 14:27). "Love one another as I have loved you. No one has greater love than to lay down one's life for one's friends" (Jn. 15:12–13).

THE ORDER OF THINGS

Remembered in Jesus Christ, the memory of God is paired with the image expressed in the Greek word *logos*. This is the cosmic song of God incarnate in the life of the world that the author of the Gospel of John writes as the prologue to his memory of God in Christ (Jn. 1:1–18).

In the beginning was the Word (the *Logos*), and the Word (the *Logos*) was with God, and the Word was God. He was in the beginning with God; All things were made through him, and without him was not anything made that was made. In him was life, and the life was the light of [all people]. (Jn. 1:1–4 KJVN).

In imagining what is meant by the word *logos* as the name for God, the writer and philosopher poet Goethe gives these words to Faust as he sits in his study translating from Greek into German the word *logos*:

"In the beginning was the Word [*das Wort*]!" But how is this known? This might be translated, "In the beginning was the Sense [*der Sinn*]!" But then is not force creative of sense? So then, "In the beginning was the Power [*die Kraft*]!" And still, what is power without act. Faust concludes to translate once more, "In the beginning was the Deed [*die Tat*]!"[6]

Word—sense—power—deed: all are distinct and united in the meaning of God as logos. As Goethe's four images convey, God as logos is the order of things known in the body as the power that creates life in time, in living and dying. This is the memory of God that the gospel of John remembers in the images of bread and wine as the body and blood of Jesus know in his life, teaching, and death, remembered as the "true light who gave power to become children of God" (Jn. 1:9,12).

John concludes his prologue with the memory of Jesus as the incarnate Word.

And the Word was made flesh and dwelt among us, and we have seen his glory, the glory as of a father's only son, full of grace and truth. . . . No one has ever seen God. It is God the only Son who is close to the Father's heart, who has made him known. (Jn. 1:14, 18, NKJV)

As the Gospel of John continues, "Jesus is 'the bread from heaven' who is 'the bread of life'" (Jn. 6:32, 35). "I am the living bread that came down from heaven. Whoever eats of this bread will live forever" (Jn. 6:51). "I am the true vine" (Jn. 15:1); and, like branch and vine, those who "abide in me and I in them bear much fruit . . . So shall those who abide in love be filled with joy (Jn. 15:4.5.9–11).

LYRIC VOICE

The Gospel of John sings this song as the cosmic song of creation and redemption in death and resurrection. Like the psalms or scripture read as a whole in the course of a liturgical year, or like the music and text in a Bach cantata set to the Sunday readings from scripture or in a Mahler symphony, the song is not built from a single musical chord to a singular narrative conclusion. This has been called the "lyric voice."[7]

Meaning is not narrowly tied to what is realized in act. Meaning is not only given in narrating the course of actions. Instead, as in poetry, images attune persons to the life of the world, to what is life, to what is, to connections and conflicts, constraints and possibilities, to what changes, sustains, dies, and remains. Narratives tell stories, but the play of images break the narrative focus on what will happen and instead attune those who have ears to hear to the rapture of particulars.[8] A concluding "amen" doesn't end the song but draws together the glory of life lived in being in time. Such is the radiant light in the music of Bach, especially in his cantatas. Similarly, the psalms provide a lyric voice that attunes those who have ears to hear. The final chords of the Psalter, 146 to 150, are notes of the glory of it all that draws all into the knowledge of eternal life in being in time.

The Christian gospels likewise offer a lyric voice that extends beyond a singular narrative of salvation that stands as a text behind the gospel texts of Matthew, Mark, Luke, and John.[9] Jesus is raised from the dead. Mary Magdalene, Mary the mother of James, and Salome arrived at the empty tomb looking for Jesus' body. A young man sitting there tells them, he is not here, he is risen. He goes before you into the wilderness of Galilee. The women believed and as true disciples go back to tell the apostles (end of story) (Mark 16:1–7).

On that same day, as the Gospel of Luke gives voice to the memory of Jesus as risen from the dead, a stranger joins the apostles on their way to Emmaus. They walk and talk together about Jesus and what has happened, about his death, and about the empty tomb, but they still do not recognize that the stranger is the risen Lord. Then over supper their eyes are opened in the breaking of the bread, just as at the last supper before Jesus' crucifixion. Bread, body, given for you (Lk. 24:30–31).

And Jesus appears to others. On the first day of the week, the Gospel of John remembers Jesus appearing to the disciples and announcing his presence with the greeting, "Peace be with you." And he tells them that they will receive the Holy Spirit, that they are called to forgive those who have persecuted them (Jn. 20:19–23); and, in response to Peter says, "Feed my sheep" (Jn. 21:15–17).

In this polyphony of voices, what emerges is the acclamation of death and resurrection remembered in bread and wine, body and blood, suffering and death, absence and presence, presence in absence, cross and resurrection. Acclamations are given in stories that break the bonds of any singular narrative rendering of the memory of God. Persons may come to believe in a singular narrative of Jesus' crucifixion and resurrection in terms of the promise of the future, in eternal life in time beyond time. However that may be, the polyphony of images and narrative renderings that form the memory of God attune and call persons in compassion, reverence, and care to what gives life in the life of the world.

PERSONAL IMAGES

In the polyphony of voices, personal images are paired with the image of God as *logos,* as "Word" calling persons into life. For Jews and Christians, God is variously described as heard and known personally in being acted upon and called to a new life. God is creator of heaven and earth (Gen. 1:1), king, ruler, governor, sustainer, judge, merciful, redeemer, father of Israel, father of us all, mother who cares for her children. God creates, orders, sustains, judges, heals, and redeems. The memory of God is given in the memory of God as personal, incarnate in the life of the world.

As H. Richard Niebuhr asked, why would impersonal images be used in imagining God instead of personal images?[10] Impersonal images suggest that humans are related to God as a matter of cause and effect. Instead, the memory of God is the memory of powers that have their own purposes, that claim humans, restrain them, and call for response. God is not a cause outside of creation but incarnate in creation as revealed in the memory of God as known and remembered in the life of the world. For Christians this is the Jewish memory of God known anew in the memory of Jesus Christ. And this is the memory of God as Holy Spirit as the memory of God incarnate in time past, revealing and calling forth what gives life in the midst of time that is the opening of the future.

THE TRINITY OF GOD

The centrality of the Christian memory of God as personal, as Father, Son, and Holy Spirit, is evidenced in the earliest account of baptism found in the late first century or early second century document titled *Didache*.[11] Persons to be received into the Christian community of faith are to be baptized in the words of the Trinitarian baptismal formula, "in the name of the Father, and of the Son, and of the Holy Spirit"[12] The Trinitarian imaging of God in the baptismal formula is further repeated in the postresurrection memory of the command of Jesus in the Gospel of Matthew: "All authority in heaven and on earth has been given to me. Go therefore and make disciples of all nations, baptizing them in the name of the Father and of the Son and of the Holy Spirit" (Matt. 28:18–19).

In the scaffolding of memory, the trinitarian imaging of God as One as Father, Son and Holy Spirit draws together and reveals the memory of God. The scaffolding of memory moves from lived experience rendered in stories and teachings to the Trinitarian images of God as One. This is the scaffolding of memory from the material of lives lived to the more formal personal images signifying the powers and purposes that form life as Father, Son, and Holy Spirit to the most formal images of God as One.

Formally, God as One is the power and the purpose that forms what it is to be. The personal image of God as Father has traditionally drawn together in memory what orders life and, thereby, forms life, creates, governs, and sustains life. The personal image of God as Son has traditionally drawn together memories of what gives life in God, that reveal what heals and reconciles, saves and gives new life in the midst of suffering limitations, sins, and injustices. As One together with Father and Son, the image of God as the Holy Spirit draws together the memories of God into the future in what gives life and creates new life opened to the future in life together as one in many, many in one.

FAITH IN BELIEVING

To know God is not to identify Christian faith in the knowledge of God with the claim of a biblical theology of salvation that stands behind different memories of God and life in God in order to reach a conclusion that resolves differences in terms of who is right and who is wrong, who is to be welcomed and embraced, and who is to be punished and disgraced. At the heart of faith in God is remembering what is suffered in life, what gives life together and what destroys that life, what are false hopes, what are the sins of the world, and what are the sins one bears in one's own life. In faith and fidelity to the memory of God, persons are drawn out of themselves in the love of God and one another. To give oneself to God is to forgive and to be forgiven in trust that God's will will be done. To give oneself to God is to be humbled and opened to the gift of life in wonder, love, praise, and thanksgiving.

Walter Brueggemann has described life lived in the memory of God as a movement from "being securely oriented, being painfully disoriented, and being surprisingly reoriented."[13] Cristian faith is not the object of believing as something possessed. Christian faith is a verb. The fourth century Nicene Creed begins with the words in Latin, "*Credo in unum Deum.*" I give my heart to one God."[14]

As faith, to give one's heart is not to give oneself to a set of belief about God. Faith is giving oneself, of entrusting oneself, to the Christian memory of God. F. D. Maurice said this simply in 1842. The creed is "not a certain scheme of divinity, but a name." The creed is "an act of allegiance or affiance."[15] To believe is to give oneself to God in acclamation and invocation that "God's will will be done."

RELIGION AND IDOLATRY

In confessions of faith the danger of idolatry highlights the nature of Christian faith in God given in the memory of God. As Søren Kierkegaard claimed, Christian faith is not given in a set of beliefs that consecrate human understandings of God and society. Christian faith is not an ethic as a set of moral principles and rules. Christian faith requires a leap of faith in giving up of oneself in response to a living God.[16]

Kierkegaard's voice from the nineteenth century opposing faith and the cultural Christianity of religion is heard throughout the twentieth century. In Protestant thought, this opposition between faith and religion is most notable at the end of the First World War with the publication of Karl Barth's *The Epistles to the Romans in 1918*.[17] There, Barth assailed liberal Christianity as a religion that worshiped a human idea of fulfillment in the life of the world. Its teaching was deaf to the initiative of God in judgment and grace. What has been called the crisis theology of neo-orthodoxy, Christian faith is a radical and continuing conversion of life as life revealed in judgment and grace. As known in Scripture, the word of God is the word of law and gospel. In judgment the idols that govern human life are broken open and the voice of God is heard calling for repentance in turning from the idols of faith to faith in God. H. Richard Niebuhr likewise developed his understanding of radical monotheism. As institutionalized in society, Christian faith may become above all else faith and fidelity to family, tribe, race, nation and state, science, religion, and culture.[18]

What the neo-orthodox tradition did in the recovery of the prophetic tradition addressing the cultural captivity of the church, the liturgical movement of the twentieth century did in recovery of the development of Christian communities as communities of worship as centrally celebrated in Baptism and the Eucharist. As emphasized by Eastern Orthodox Alexander Schmemann and Roman Catholic Aidan Kavanagh, Christian faith stands opposed to mystical religions, cultural Christianity, and a secular world where life is fulfilled in personal success and pleasures of one's own making. Such are the idols that set people apart from the actual life of the world. Death is denied in the consolation of belief in life beyond death. Instead, as life given in time, death is conquered in life in Christ. Christ reveals the power and truth of God as creator and redeemer in his life and teaching, death, and resurrection. This is the saving memory of Christ that is given together with others in the life of the Church lived in the memory and call of God in Christ. Celebrated and effected in prayer and worship, this is a life of "right worship" lived out in praise and adoration of God in the recognition and embrace of one another. In other words, this is life given in the love of God and love of neighbor, stranger, and friend.[19]

NOTES

1. For a comprehensive commentary and bibliography on the psalms, see Walter Brueggemann and William Bellinger Jr., *Psalms. The New Cambridge Bible Commentary* (New York: Cambridge University Press, 2014). On the development of the place of the psalms in Christian liturgical traditions from monastic communities to cathedral worship to daily worship, see the multiple authored entries under "Daily Prayer" in *The New Westminster Dictionary of Liturgy & Worship,* ed. Paul Bradshaw (Louisville, KY: Westminster John Knox, 2002), 140–50.

2. Dietrich Bonhoeffer, *Psalms: The Prayer Book of the Bible* (Minneapolis, MN: Augsburg, 1970); Martin Luther, "Preface to the Psalter, Luther's Works, vol. 35, ed. E. Theodore Backman (Philadelphia: Muhlenberg, 1960), 254 where Luther speaks of the psalms as "the little Bible."

3. On the polyphony of scripture and the psalms, see Gordon Lathrop, *Saving Images, the Presence of the Bible in Christian Liturgy* (Minneapolis, MN: 2017), 39–40. Also, see Walter Brueggemann, *Theology of The Old Testament: Testimony, Dispute, Advocacy, Second Edition* (Minneapolis, MN: Fortress Press, 2005). Especially helpful is Brueggemann's account of the development of biblical criticism and theology in moving from seeking a text of objective historical and theological truths revealed behind the text to the world of the texts and in their reception their polyphonic testimonies in the life of the world.

4. English translations drawn from translations from the King James Bible as adopted in the morning office of morning prayer in the Episcopal Church in *The Book of Common Prayer* (New York: Church Publishing, 1979).

5. As central to Gordon's Lathrop's liturgical theology, see *Holy Things: A Liturgical Theology* (Minneapolis, MN: Fortress Press,1993), 19–20; and *Saving Images,* 39–40.

6. Johann Wolfgang von Goethe, *Faust* (The Project Gutenberg EBook of Faust, 2007), J. Studirzimmer, lines 47–60, online at gutenberg.org/files/21000/2100-h/21000-h.htm.

7. See *The Lyric Theory Reader: A Critical Anthology,* eds. Virginia Jackson and Yopie Prins (Baltimore: Johns Hopkins University Press, 2014), their introductory essay, "Phenomenologies of Lyric Reading," 382–89, and Martin Heidegger, "Poetically Man Dwells," 390–99.

8. See Charles Altieri, *The Particulars of Rapture: An Aesthetics of the Affects* (Ithaca, NY: Cornell University Press, 2003), 1–36 on an aesthetic theory of meaning.

9. On the play of images and narrative renderings of the resurrection that are given in the gospels themselves, see, for example, Norman Perrin, *The Resurrection According to Matthew, Mark, and Luke* (Philadelphia: Fortress Press, 1977).

10. H. Richard Niebuhr, *Radical Monotheism and Western Culture*, with supplementary essays (Louisville, KY: Westminster/John Knox, 1943, 1952, 1955, 1960), 44–48.

11. *Didache,* tr. and commentary, Aaron Milavec (Collegeville, MN: Liturgical Press, 2003).

12. Ibid., 7:2.

13. Walter Brueggemann, *Praying the Psalms* (Eugene, OR: Cascade Books, 2007), 2.

14. Greek, Latin, and English translation of the Nicene Creed are variously available online. On the etymology of "credo" see Online Etymology Dictionary at https://www.etymonline.com/word/credo.

15. Frederick Denison Maurice, *The Kingdom of Christ*, ed. Alex R. Vidler (London: SCM Press, 1958), vol. 2:20.

16. Søren Kierkegaard, *Fear and Trembling,* tr. Walter Lowrie (Princeton, NJ: Princeton University Press, 2013*),*

17. Karl Barth, *The Epistle to the Romans,* tr. Edwin C. Hoskyns (London: Oxford, 1933).

18. H. Richard Niebuhr, *The Kingdom of God in American* (Chicago: Willet, Clark & Co., 1937), 193; and *Radical Monotheism*, 49–89.

19. Alexander Schmemann, "Worship in a Secular Age," *For the Life of the World,* (Crestwood, NY: St. Vladimir's Seminary Press, 1963), 17–134; Aidan Kavanagh, *On Liturgical Theology* (New York: Pueblo, 1984), 151–79. On the twentieth-century liturgical movement, see Keith F. Pecklers, et al., "The Liturgical Movement," *The New Westminster Dictionary of Liturgy and Worship*, ed. Paul Bradshaw (Louisville, KY: Westminster John Knox, 2002), 285–89.

Chapter Four

Sacrament: Incarnate Memory

In offering an account of Christian faith in light of understanding Christian communities as communities of worship, Aidan Kavanagh argued what is needed is an account of how God is known in worship.[1] This he claimed could not be an account of liturgy as given in beliefs about God as expressed in the elements of liturgy since beliefs arose from these communities. As the knowledge of God, a theology of liturgy must be an account of how God is known in worship and therein confessed in Christian beliefs.

LEX ORANDI LEX CREDENDI

Often cited is the claim that knowledge of God is given in prayer, expressed by the fifth century maxim, *"lex orandi, lex credendi,"* translated as "the law of praying is the law of believing." How the one is the other, however, is expressed by the full statement of Prosper of Aquitaine: *"legume credendi lex statuat supplicandi."*[2] What is significant in understanding this maxim is what is claimed by the past, imperfect, subjunctive verb *statuat*.

Statuat is not the present tense of the verb "to be," where prayer and beliefs are one another. Instead, *legume credendi* is spoken of first followed by the passive imperfect subjunctive verb s*tatuat* followed by the word *supplicandi*. *Statuat* has at its root the establishment of something as in the case of setting up a statue. Christian faith is established, grounded, and formed in the lives of those who are supplicants, who in prayer and worship give themselves to God. Kavanagh writes,

> The verb *statuat* subordinates the law of belief to the law of worship in just the same way, and for just the same reasons, as our reception of God's Word is subordinated to the presentation of that Word to us in the act of its being revealed and proclaimed to us. Belief is always consequent upon encounter with the Source of the grace of faith. Therefore, Christians do not worship because they

believe. They believe because the One in whose gift faith lies is regularly met in the act of communal worship.[3]

WORSHIP, MEMORY, AND RITUAL

In speaking of the memory of God in worship, we are speaking about a ritual process that forms human life.[4] As ritual, worship in its order and regularity forms the scaffolding of the memory of God as received by those who worship. In worship, the memory of God is an object of consciousness as perceived in word and act in the presence and actions of those gathered in worship.[5] In turn, to speak about the memory of God is to speak about the memory of God as one's own, as received subjectively (by the subject).[6]

Together, the memory of God is objectively given and subjectively received where what is perceived as an object of consciousness is paired with the subject's memories that make sense of a person's own life in the life of the world. The memory of God may make sense given in comfort and confirmation of life as known; or it may be cause of doubt, questioning, and reimagining what is good and true, what to do and be together and as oneself.

What is celebrated and effected in worship is the encounter and knowledge of God.[7] As the memory of God, these are memories of powers and purposes that form life, that give life. These are memories that attune those who worship in the life of the world and call for response. These are the memories that draw persons out of themselves into the life of the world, especially evident in worship in moments of change that are turning points in life.

For example, such is the power of services of marriage where two persons give themselves to each other in the promise to love and care for one another all the days of their life. And such is the power of gathering at the times of death in worship and remembrance in thanksgiving for the life of another, for lament at our loss, and in acclamation of the grace of God in the resurrection of the dead and the communion saints. Such also is the power of daily prayers in giving thanks, in the confession of faults and failures, in remembrance for the gifts of other, in prayers for those in need, in prayers for the grace of God and the hope of the world. And such is the Christian memory of God that came to be centrally celebrated in the Eucharist.

EUCHARISTIC MEMORY

After the death of Jesus, in what have come to be called house churches, Jewish Christians gathered to share a meal, pray, and share memories of the life and teachings of Jesus.[8] From these beginnings, the memory of God in

Christ was celebrated in what came to be called the Eucharist. Two texts from the time of the early church provide a picture of what becomes central in the development of the memory of God and Christ celebrated in the Eucharist in different communities in different times and places, with different challenges and concerns, in different cultures and across cultures.

As expressed in the Didache—whether written in the last half of the first century, at the turn of the century, or sometime in the first half of the second century—in gathering in the celebration of the Eucharist the meal shared is paired with the memories of Jesus' life and teachings, death and resurrection. As a book of teachings (hence the title, *Didache*), the author writes,

> Now concerning the Eucharist, give thanks this way. First, concerning the cup: We thank thee, our Father, for the holy vine of David Thy servant, which You made known to us through Jesus Thy Servant; to Thee be the glory for ever. And concerning the broken bread: We thank Thee, our Father, for the life and knowledge which You made known to us through Jesus Thy Servant; to Thee be the glory for ever. Even as this broken bread was scattered over the hills, and was gathered together and became one, so let Thy Church be gathered together from the ends of the earth into Thy kingdom; for Thine is the glory and the power through Jesus Christ forever.

In conclusion after communion, the author offers a final prayer of thanksgiving to be prayed.

> We thank Thee, holy Father, for Thy holy name which You did cause to tabernacle in our hearts, and for the knowledge and faith and immortality, which You made known to us through Jesus Thy Servant; to Thee be the glory for ever. Thou, Master almighty, didst create all things for Thy name's sake; You gave food and drink to men for enjoyment, that they might give thanks to Thee; but to us You did freely give spiritual food and drink and life eternal through Thy Servant. Before all things we thank Thee that You are mighty; to Thee be the glory for ever. Remember, Lord, Thy Church, to deliver it from all evil and to make it perfect in Thy love, and gather it from the four winds, sanctified for Thy kingdom which Thou have prepared for it; for Thine is the power and the glory for ever. Let grace come, and let this world pass away. Hosanna to the God (Son) of David! If any one is holy, let him come; if any one is not so, let him repent. Maranatha. Amen.
>
> *The Didache*[9]

In the middle of the second century, in an apology addressed to the Roman Emperor arguing against persecution, Justin wrote, however idealized, another, different description of the Eucharist and in that a description of Christian faith and life.

Over all that we take to eat we bless the creator of all things through God's Son Jesus Christ and through the Holy Spirit. And on that day named after the sun all, whether they live in the city or the countryside, [all] are gathered together in unity. Then the records of the apostles or the writings of the prophets are read for as long as there is time. When the reader has concluded, the presider in a discourse admonishes and invites us into the pattern of these good things. Then we all stand together and offer prayer. . . . when we have concluded the prayer, bread is set out to eat, together with wine and water. The presider likewise offers up prayer and thanksgiving, as much as he can, and the people sing out their assent saying the *amen*. There is a distribution of the things over which thanks have been said and each person participates, and these things are sent by the deacons to those who are not present. Those who are prosperous and who desire to do so, give what they wish, according to each one's own choice and the collection is deposited with the presider. He aids orphans and widows, those who are in want through disease or through another cause, those who are in prison, and foreigners who are sojourning here. In short, the presider is a guardian to all those who are in need.

Justin, 1st Apology[10]

IN CREATION AND REDEMPTION

Reflected in the Didache and in Justin's account of the Eucharist, at the center of the Christian memory of God is the goodness of life in the life of the world.[11] As in the Jewish memory of God, the memory of God was given in a thanksgiving prayer said before a meal and in remembrance of God as creator of all things as celebrated on the Sabbath. This was in memory the acclamation given in the account of creation that begins the book of Genesis. In the memory of God, these are thanksgivings for life in the life of the world, for being in time.

The memory of Jesus in the early gatherings over a meal together is also the memory of God breaking into time. Alongside the memory of being in time, this is the eucharistic memory of God acting in history. In the Didache these are memories of Jesus as God's servant, as bearer of the hope of the kingdom of God as prayed in the Lord's Prayer. In Justin's apology these are memories given in the voices of apostles and prophets. And in the early Christian communities, this is the celebration of the Easter Passover and of new life in Christ in the celebration of Pentecost.[12]

Together in the pairing of a meal shared together with life in Christ, the Eucharist is a prayer of thanksgiving to God for the gifts and blessings of creation given in time, in life together, in good times and in times of tribulation, in love and care, in one generation to another. This is the memory of God as incarnate in the life of the world, as the source and renewal of life. This is cause of praise and thanksgiving that in remembrance the memory of God continues to call those who remember into life. This is the Jewish prophetic memory of God taken up in the saving memory of Christ.

SIN AND SALVATION

The memory of God and of life in God given in creation is also a clouded or stained memory. The memory of life in God is captive to sin and the sins of the world. Idols shine. Love and desires are corrupted, captive, or lost. Such is the desire to be the ruler of one's life, to use one's power for oneself, to secure one's power and pleasure, one's goals, individual and corporate, personal and tribal. "Vanities of vanities, says the Teacher, vanities of vanities! All is vanity" (Eccl. 1:2).

In the Jewish and Christian memory of the story of creation in the Garden of Eden, this is the fall from grace and the loss of the tree of life (Gen. 2:4–3:24). And still, this is the memory of hope and promise of the fullness of life imaged as the covenant between God and the those who remember and follow in the way of God. In sin and salvation, these are memories of judgement and repentance, forgiveness and grace. This is the memory of God as creator and father of us all, this is the memory of Christ as bearer of the kingdom of God, and this is the memory of the Holy Spirit who acts upon us now, that is the memory of life given together as the people of God in being drawn out of themselves in compassion, recognition, and care of one another. This is the gift of the Holy Spirit known together in the life of the church as grounded in prayer and worship.

IN TIME AND MEMORY

For Jews and Christians, God is the god of history who is known in time. The memory of God is an ongoing conversation and conversion given in what is remembered as God incarnate in life and as God acting in history (to use these two different metaphors) that now calls for response.

As the nature of memory is given in time, so is the Christian memory of God known in time. Given in time, this is the call of knowing what claims one and knowing that one doesn't know what will come to be. This is the memory of the call of Abraham to leave home with Sarah with the hope and promise of finding a new home where family might prosper in a new land of their own (Gen. 12–22). This is the call of Jacob's wrestling with an angel through the night until the beginning of the new day, asking for a blessing and receiving a blessing but not the name of God (Gen. 34:24–29). And this is the memory of the call to Moses from God from a burning bush to lead the people out of slavery in Egypt (Ex. 3:1–15). This is God who is remembered as giving his name only as I Am—or in other words, in present and future tense, "I AM who I AM" and "I will be who I will be" (Ex. 3:14), expressed in writing only by the tetragrammaton theonym transliterated in English as YHWH.

Such are the memories of the call to the prophets as a call from the heavens in the power and glory of the holy, in the sight of angels and creatures, in fire and light and in response "woe is me" (Is. 6–1–5); or as a call "not in the wind . . . not in the earthquake . . . not in the fire . . . [but in a] still small voice" (1Kgs. 19:11–12).

Together, the voices of scripture and of the tradition, the voices of the present assembly and the voices of the world form a polyphony of voices. These voices form the memory and call of God into the life of the world beyond what is claimed and desired at any one time.

Together in prayer and worship, in the voices of many the memory of God is acclaimed and examined, examined and acclaimed in conversation with others. Given in time, the memory of God attunes persons to the presence of God in the life of the world. Given in time, the call of God is the call to discern what is central to the memory of God and what that calls for in suffering the limitations and possibilities in a particular time and place.

THE SHAPE OF THE LITURGY

Celebrated in the Eucharist, the shape of Christian faith as the memory and call of God is imaged in the shape of the liturgy. Like the polyphony of the voices in scripture, together different images of the shape of the liturgy reflect what Christian communities and their members share together and what distinguishes differences in their memories of God and the life into which they are called.

Taking, Blessing, Breaking, Sharing

In moving from the liturgical actions forming the Eucharist to the shape of the liturgy that celebrates and forms Christian faith and life, Anglican Dominican Gregory Dix described the shape of the liturgy as "taking, blessing, breaking, and sharing."[13] For Dix, Christian faith is a matter of giving oneself to God as redeemer of the world as revealed in Jesus' life, teaching, ministry, death, and resurrection. Jesus is Christ, the Messiah, the anointed one, the bearer of the saving life in God calling humans into that life. Christ is God incarnate revealing what it means to live a godly life, to live life into God, what the Orthodox tradition speaks of as *theosis,* as participation in sharing in the life of God.[14]

The central image of Christian faith for Dix is given in the Greek word *kenosis.* Jesus empties himself in life in God (Phil. 2:7). He entrusts himself to God in his life and in his death: "into your hands I commend my spirit" (Lk. 23:45). Imaged in the word *agape,* this is giving oneself up entirely to life in the love God as God has given himself to the world (Jn. 3:16). This is the shape of the liturgy as the shape of life given as the love of God and neighbor.

Right Worship

In imaging the shape of the liturgy, Orthodox theologian Alexander Schmemann offers the image of "right worship."[15] The image of "right worship" is meant to convey that worship is not the right performance of the Eucharist any more than it is right actions of the moral life. What is celebrated in the shape of the liturgy of the Eucharist is for the life of the world. Such is the love of God that is known in Christ as love incarnate in the life of the world.[16]

Initiation and Incorporation

Given the historical recovery of the centrality of Baptism and the Eucharist as together the central liturgical rites forming Christian worship, Aidan Kavanagh images the shape of the liturgy in terms of "initiation and incorporation." What is centrally expressed in Baptism and celebrated in the Eucharist is initiation and incorporation in life together in the life of God in the world as it was meant to be over and against the abnormality of the way of the world.[17]

Gathering and Sending

More recently, Gordon Lathrop has described the shape of the radical conversion of life celebrated together in Baptism and the Eucharist as "gathering leading to sending because of word next to meal."[18] Materially, Christians gather for worship together; listen to scripture read and preached; offer prayers and songs, confessions of sins and acclamations of forgiveness; and conclude in gathering around a table to share a meal in the memory of God in Christ and in that are called out into the life of the world.

Together Dix, Schmemann, Kavanagh, and Lathrop image Christian faith in the shape of the liturgy as a matter of the love of God in giving oneself to

God in being called together as one in gathering and sending into the life of the world in love. What is distinctive about Lathrop's focus is his focus on the polyphony of voices that form the memory and call of God. The shape of the liturgy that is the shape of Christian faith and life is both shared as one as God is One and many as lived out in the world.

Thanksgiving and Beseeching

In review of the work in liturgical theology in understandings of the shape of the liturgy, Don Saliers describes the practices of prayer that form the shape of the liturgy in terms of a set of verbs: praise and thanksgiving, invoking and beseeching, lamenting, confessing, and interceding.[19] The liturgical prayers of worship reflect the polyphony of voices that form the memory of God. They offer praise and give thanks for the blessings of life; pray that God's will be done; lament in sorrow over the loss of what is loved and what is destroyed by the violence of the world; repent in confessing the sins they bear in the world in which they live; and remember and pray for one another.

Like the voices of scripture, liturgical worship as the order of prayer in the life of the Christian community gives voice to the memory and call of God in one's own life. As prayed, the many voices in prayer and worship are sometimes in harmony and sometimes dissonant as they call out the deepest longings and acclamations of the heart that call into question the words of one's mouth and what a person truly believes (gives themselves to) in their hearts. In praise and thanksgiving, invocation and beseeching, lamenting, confessing, and interceding, in prayer Christian faith is a continuing conversion of the memory and call of faith and life in God in the life of the world.[20] Together with the other images of the shape of the liturgy as the shape of Christian faith and life, the shape of the liturgy may be imaged as "faith in believing."

Other Voices

The strength and limitation of imaging the shape of the liturgy and the prayers of the people is that the memory of God celebrated and formed in worshipping is always more than what is imaged. Images may be idealized, objectified in terms of an idea beyond change, beyond time. Human actions may likewise be detailed as the nature of the end. The danger of imaging the shape of the liturgy, however, is not only a problem of idolatry where an image or set of images are paired singularly to a particular set of intentions and actions.

The further danger in imagining the shape of the liturgy as believing—as what it is to give oneself in faith to God—is the absence of other images that reflect the memory and call of God in different Christian communities. What is especially lost are the voices of those who have been oppressed, especially in the histories and theologies of the established churches. Only together in the different voices and accounts of the memory and call of God do we hear what has been lost from view that is needed to hear the memory of God calling persons in life together.

The Memory of Others

The narrowing of Christian voices increased as Christianity became the established religion of the Roman Empire in the fourth century and, subsequently, as Protestant churches became the established religions of the new European nations and continued following the separation of church and state where old and new churches were still quasi-established by the people of a nation.

Where established or quasi-established, Christian faith was narrowed as a matter of beliefs and actions institutionalized in the life and teachings of the church. Together as established or as quasi-established, church and state, religion and culture informed each other, sometimes challenged each other, but almost always supported one another. Church and state were twinned together in forming a sacred canopy of beliefs and practices.[21] Universities, colleges, and seminaries reflected and supported the dominant society. From these institutions came those who wrote the Christian histories and theologies as the established truths of the established churches. The voices of those outside the establishment were marginalized, at the margins of the established order of things.

However, unrecognized by those who ruled, there were still those who heard the stories of Jesus and the prophetic voices in the Bible. They heard different voices that formed their memory of God as a saving memory. For example, they heard the Jewish memory of God as wandering Arameans, refugees, enslaved, freed with hope and the promise of peace and prosperity, and yet again suffering the violence of injustice. In their suffering they felt recognized and embraced in the love of God in Jesus' life, teaching, and ministry, in the voice of God calling for justice, in Jesus' suffering death on the cross, and in faith in the resurrection in the promise of new life together breaking in upon them, already and not yet.

These are missing memories of God. These are voices that speak of where the grace of life is given juxtaposed to (and in judgment against) those consumed by the privileged life they live, unable to hear the prophetic voice of God calling those who are imprisoned in their world into a new life in life in Christ.

Lift Every Voice and Sing

Missing voices from the established histories of Christian faith and life have included anabaptist and monastic memories of the way of Christ as the way of peace in sharing in life together, founded in prayer and worship and given in the renunciation of the use of violence. Other voices that have been missing are the colonized, enslaved, oppressed and disenfranchised, reformers and revolutionaries, aboriginal or first peoples, African Americans, racial minorities, refugees and immigrants, women, persons with different sexual identities, and those otherwise marginalized, often tied to poverty and social class.

The memory of God of the oppressed and marginalized may be drawn together by different images that give voice to the shape of the liturgy that, as in the polyphony of scripture, may deepen what is celebrated and effected in worship. For example, receiving Christian faith as slaves, many African Americans recognized themselves enslaved as the Israelites were enslaved in Egypt, called to freedom from captivity by the power of God, born anew in covenant with God, bearing the promise of freedom in life lived together in fidelity to that promise. In Jesus they recognized themselves as suffering servants, suffering the sins of the world, that in bearing suffering in love they were saved by Christ, that in Christ they were blessed in the call of justice that is love and saved from the hate that destroys the love that redeems.

African American worship, of course, is not one thing. It variously develops along different lines ranging from Evangelical and Pentecostal traditions of worship to Anglican and Roman Catholic sacramental traditions. How worship in these different communities of worship might be framed in terms of the shape of the liturgy—and in that how Christian faith is celebrated and known—may certainly be imaged in different ways. One set of images that express the shape of the liturgy as known in their worship together is imaged from James Weldon Johnson's song titled "Lift Every Voice and Sing."

Composed in 1900 in celebration of Abraham Lincoln's birthday, the first image, "lift every voice," and the second image, "sing," provide formal images that together image the shape of the liturgy and the shape of life in God and Christ celebrated in African American communities of faith.[22] "Lift every voice and sing," hear every voice, gather together every voice and sing. Know that we are not alone; hear and be called in liberty to be true to our memory of God in hope and the promise that we may "ever stand, true to our God, true to our native land."[23]

ONE IN MANY

Taking, blessing, breaking, and sharing; worship; initiation and incorporation; gathering and sending; faith in believing; lift every voice and sing. Such are images that together celebrate the shape of the liturgy. In the memory of God as Father, Son, and Holy Spirit, this is the continuing song of what gives life. This is the song of compassion that is the song of justice, that already and not yet stands in critique of false promises and actions and sends those who believe into the life of the world in love. Therein the grace of God is known in life together with one another as the people of God, already and not yet.

In such faith and fidelity to the memory of God, Christians are attuned to the life of the world in ways that are shared and individuated. What they see and feel, what they hear and how they respond is imaged as one in many.

What they share in the newness of life together, Paul speaks in the language of virtue. "Idolatry, sorcery, enmities, strife, jealousy, anger, quarrels, dissensions, [and] factions" are cast aside by "the fruit of the Spirit as love, joy, peace, patience, kindness, generosity, faithfulness, gentleness, and self-control" (Gal. 5:20–23). Faith as entrusting oneself to the memory of God known together in worship is to give oneself to God breaking into the present in love. In such love is faith formed and reformed in hope in the call to love incarnate in the time and place of one's own life.

NOTES

1. Aidan Kavanagh, *On Liturgical Theology* (New York: Pueblo, 1987), 87–88.

2. On Prosper of Aquitaine and the origin and meaning of *lex orandi lex credendi*, see Gordon Lathrop, *Holy People: A Liturgical Ecclesiology* (Minneapolis: Augsburg Fortress, 1999), 102–4.

3. Kavanagh, *On Liturgical Theology*, 91.

4. On the nature of ritual, see Roy A. Rappaport, *Ritual and Religion in the Making of Humanity* (Cambridge: Cambridge University Press, 1999), 24–58, beginning with his definition of ritual as "the performance of more or less invariant sequences of formal acts and utterances not entirely encoded by the performers." In terms of Christian worship as ritual, the more or less invariant character of ritual establishes a world in which persons participate and make their own.

5. On the ritual elements central to Christian worship, see Kavanagh, *On Liturgical Theology*, 140–42.

6. On the distinction between objective and subjective contexts of meaning in understanding socially mediated provinces of meaning, see Schutz, *The Phenomenology of the Social World*, 132–38. Drawing on Schutz's social phenomenology, see, Peter L. Berger and Thomas Luckmann, *The Social Construction of Reality* (Garden City, NY: Anchor Books, 1967).

7. See Kavanagh, *On Liturgical Theology,* 137–39.

8. For a concise summary of Hellenistic household associations and the developments of Christian communities of faith, with references to current literature, see Gordon W. Lathrop, *Saving Images,* 57–58, 109–12. Among the references, see Dennis E. Smith, *From Symposium to Eucharist: The Banquet in the Early Christian World* (Minneapolis, MN: Fortress, 2003). Also see Carolyn Ann Osiek and David L. Balch, *Families in the New Testament World: Households and House Churches* (Philadelphia: Westminster/John Knox, 1997).

9. *Didache,* tr. J. B. Lightfoot, Early Christian Writings, online at https://www.earlychristianwritings.com, ch, 9–10.

10. Justin, *1 Apology,* 67, tr. Gordon W. Lathrop, *Holy Things: A Liturgical Theology* (Minneapolis: Augsburg Fortress, 1993), 45.

11. See Schmemann, *Introduction to Liturgical Theology* (Crestwood, NY: St.Vladimire's Seminary Press), 41–45 to 68 on the Eucharist in relation to time and creation,

12. Ibid., 68–89.

13. Dom Gregory Dix, *The Shape of the Liturgy* (New York: Seabury Press, 1982), *beginning* with his initial claim of the shape of the liturgy, 48–50.

14. On theosis see Vigen Guroian, "Love That Is Divine and Human," *The Orthodox Reality: Culture, Theology, and Ethics in the Modern World* (Grand Rapids, MI: Baker Academic, 107–22. Reflecting the Anglican exemplary tradition, see Timothy F. Sedgwick, "The Anglican Exemplary Tradition," *Anglican Theological Review* 94 (Spring 2012) 2:207–31.

15. On the nature of worship as "right worship" see Schmemann on the liturgical movement, *Introduction to Liturgical Theology,* 13–15, 27–29, *and* Kavanagh, *On Liturgical Theology,* 60–61.

16. See especially Schmemann, *For the Life of the World: Sacraments and Orthodoxy* (Crestwood, NY: St. Vladimir's Seminary Press, 1965), concluding on sacrament and symbol, 138. On incarnate love see Vigen Guroian, "Love That Is Divine and Human," *The Orthodox Reality: Culture Theology, and Ethics in the Modern World* (Grand Rapids, MI: Baker Academic, 2018), 107–22.

17. Kavanagh, On Liturgical Theology, 166–69. As initiated leading to incorporation celebrated in baptism, see Kavanagh, *The Shape of Baptism: The Rite of Christian Initiation* (New York: Pueblo Publishing, 1978), 159–63.

18. Lathrop, *Saving Images,* 99–101.

19. Don E. Saliers, *Worship as Theology: Foretaste of Glory Divine* (Nashville, TN: Abingdon, 1994).

20. Saliers, esp. chap. 9, "Beyond the Text: The Symbolic Languages of Liturgy," 139–53.

21. Still insightful on the continued cultural establishment of religion given the nature of churches as voluntary associations in secular societies marked by the separation of church and state is H. Richard Niebuhr's classic study, The Social Sources of Denominationalism (New York: Henry Holt, 1929).

22. *Lift Every Voice and Sing II: An African American Hymnal* (New York: Church Publishing, 1993) and its introduction, Harold T. Lewis, "Why an African American Hymnal?," xii–xvi.

23. To paraphrase from the first hymn of *Lift Every Voice and Sing*, titled *"Lift Every Voice and Sing."*

Chapter Five

Assembly: Many in One

From their beginnings in the first century, Christian communities and their members differed in thought and act. These were differences born in the cradle of civilizations, in Mesopotamia and around the Mediterranean Sea in what would become the Roman Empire. Differences in thought, in religious practices, and in ways of being in the world reflect differences in life among subsistence farmers, towns, cities, and empires; differences in positions in society, wealth and class; and given the range of different religions and cultures. These have been variously described in contrasting images, for example, the difference between the enchanted world of paganism and mystery religions to the monotheistic faith of Judaism and Christianity, revealing a universal moral order.[1]

Christian faith, however, in its beginning is no one such thing but the faith of different communities given in different memories of God that came together in the memory of God known in the life of the Church as a community of worship. This memory was itself born from the life of churches and monastic communities.

MONASTIC COMMUNITIES

Christian solitary ascetics, remembered as the desert fathers, were Christians who came largely from village churches to follow the words of Jesus: "If you would be perfect, go, sell what you possess and give to the poor, and you will have treasure in heaven; and come, follow me" (Matt. 19:21). The first community linking cells of solitary monks together into monastic communities was created in upper Egypt along the Nile River in 320. Formed in prayer and work together—expressed in the later Benedictine Latin maxim, *ora et labora* (pray and work)—these monasteries begun by Pachomius came to include seven thousand monks. Further north along the Mediterranean in Caesarea, Basil of Caesarea gathered with others on his family estate to form a monastic community centered in prayer and serving those in need, including caring for the sick and dying.[2]

What we know of the monastic life from these first beginnings is limited, largely known from what can be discerned from the first monastic rules of Pachomius and of Basil[3] that became the primary sources for the development of "The Rule of St. Benedict" approximately 200 years later in 534.[4] What can be said is that the early Christian monastic communities were centered in a life of poverty and simplicity, in prayer, in singing of psalms, and in hearing the reading of scripture.

MONASTIC LIFE

As ascetics, from the Greek meaning exercise or discipline, poverty is a discipline (*áskēsis*) marked by a simple diet and periods of fasting to purge the body of desire of needs and pleasures. Work is a matter of making provisions for the necessities of common life, from field to kitchen, in selling what is simply made and buying what is simply needed, in providing welcome to strangers and care to those in need. Work is not to take the place of prayer. Prayer is to fill the life of work and, as ordered in the course of each day, in hearing the reading of scripture, in the singing of psalms, and in praying to God.

Other practices focused on the examination of one's life. This included the practice of making an oral confession of sins to another. In confession, what is falsely loved is known as named, that it may be repented, turned away from in turning to what is truly loved. More broadly, prayers of thanksgiving and intercession form memory and focus attention on what gives life. Above all, central to the practice of holiness was the celebration of the Eucharist. Monasticism was not a faith in life of God as opposed to the Church. Monasticism was formed by those seeking a deepening and renewal of the memory and presence of God.[5]

THE MONASTIC CHALLENGE

As a renewal movement, monasticism witnessed to a radically different life in Christ from those who were members of the churches but had lost what others sought as the presence of God apart from life shaped by the desires, ambitions, and necessities that form life in society. So, it seemed to many, as Bernard McGinn writes, "Monasticism virtually alone provided the context within which some Christians could cultivate the knowledge of scripture and the life of penance and prayer that prepared the believer for more special forms of immediate contact with God in this life." In these practices, concludes McGinn, monks could come to be "considered the only 'real' Christians."[6]

What is surprising is that instead of forming two separate communities of faith, the developing churches and monastic communities came together in the fourth century to form the Church as a communion of Christian communities that recognized each other in sharing together common worship and a confession of faith in one God, Father, Son, and Holy Spirit. Instead of many, the Church was formed as one. What is not surprising is that it was monastic leaders who became the teachers and bishops of Christian communities of faith who were central to the formation of the Church as one.

THE CHURCH AS ONE

Differences among Christian communities have been largely interpreted historically in terms of different claims about Christian beliefs about God and the knowledge of God revealed in Jesus. As in Adolph von Harnack's *History of Dogma* written in 1894,[7] differences in beliefs have provided the primary framework or reference point for understanding Christian faith and the history of Christianity until the recovery of early historical documents and archaeological discoveries that made possible subsequent social, historical accounts of late antiquity and Christianity in the rise of the Roman Empire.[8] Whether Roman Catholic or Protestant, Eastern Orthodoxy, Anabaptist, or Pentecostal and Evangelical free churches, the faiths of each have been viewed as matters of different beliefs about Jesus' life and teachings and how they were understood, received, and taught. Competing claims were argued in terms of what is true and false, faith and heresy, faithfulness and apostasy.

Understanding Christian faith as it was received and passed on in the churches of the early Roman Empire, East and West, is not, however, a matter of right beliefs but a matter of the development of the Church as one in many as formed and celebrated in baptism and the Eucharist, in prayer and worship, and in the practices of faith. This is the story of the emergence of the Church in the wedding together of the devotional and spiritual practices of monasticism and the Eucharistic celebration of the churches of the empire.[9]

In becoming bishops in the developing churches, these early Church leaders brought together the devotional piety and spiritual practices formed in Hellenistic and Christian schools and in monastic communities with the Eucharist worship of the churches celebrating Christ and the coming of the kingdom of God in judgment and salvation. Together, Christian faith was giving oneself in trust in and fidelity to spiritual practices of faith centered in the Christian community of worship centered itself in the Eucharist.[10]

THE ADEPTS

What stands at the center of this history are the fathers (and mothers[11]) of the Church who were born to the landed aristocracy. Males, such as Basil of Caesarea, were schooled at home by tutors in preparation to govern as leaders of the aristocracy. At home they gained fluency in languages, in reading and writing. Schooled in spiritual practices at Hellenistic and Christian schools, they spent additional time in monastic communities. Monastically formed, they came to be recognized as holy, wise in the way of faith. These are those the Patristic scholar Richard Norris called adepts.[12] They bore the mantle of leaders with skills to teach and rule in the life of Christian communities, in churches and in monastic communities. Those such as Basil preached, taught others, and came to represent the nascent church in forming the teachings and practices of Christian faith as a shared faith expressed most fully in the celebration of the Eucharist.

PRACTICES OF FAITH

While spiritual practices have been identified with Hellenistic schools of thought, especially Stoicism and Epicureanism, disciplined practices forming thought and desire were central to Jewish and Christian faith. Spiritual practices of Christian faith inhere in prayer and worship. Together they form the scaffolding of the memory of God that attunes persons to the polyphony of voices in awareness of what others suffer and what gives life in their lives.

As it was for those in Hellenistic schools, Christian schools, and monastic communities, spiritual practices are embodied practices of the body and the mind that together examine human desire. Grounded in embodied act, imaged and formed in thought, spiritual practices focus and form attention in the examination and reception of the memory of God.

In the first century CE, Philo of Alexandria provides two lists of spiritual practices. The first list is translated as that of research, thorough investigation, reading, listening, attention, self-mastery, indifference to indifferent things, and the accomplishment of duties. The second list is translated as reading, meditation, therapies of the passion, and remembrance of good things.[13]

While variously named in forming the human person in attunement and response to the world, spiritual practices forming the memory of God may be imaged as practices of the mind, as ascetical practices of the body, and as moral practices in the life of the world that together form the memory and call of God.

Practices of the Mind

The word "examination" may seem to be too strong a word to describe spiritual practices of the mind. To examine too easily conveys the sense of judgments about what is true. However, more basically, to examine has meant to question, to test, to draw out the truth of something, etymologically from the Latin to draw out or to draw forth.[14] To examine is to remember what has been suffered, what breaks in upon oneself, to recognize loss and limitations, challenges and opportunities, relations to family, friends, neighbors, and strangers, what is the cause of sorrow and lament, and what is the source of joy and gladness. To examine is to reflect on one's own life, to call to memory what one has done and what has been left undone that has turned one away from what gives life.

To examine is to remember in reflection what makes sense and what makes nonsense, to feel in memory what is joy in life, what is loved, what it is to be loved, to know what it is to love rightly. As Augustine addresses God in in beginning his *Confessions*, "In yourself you rouse us, giving us delight in glorifying you, because you made us with yourself as our goal, and our heart is restless until it rests in you."[15]

Meditation and Examination

Tied together with physical and moral practices, meditation and contemplation are spiritual practices of the mind. Together they examine and form memory. In the strict sense of the word, to meditate comes from the Latin root meaning "to measure." To meditate is to focus attention in the examination of one thing: a feeling, a word, a phrase, a text, an image, a story, a claim, a question. Contemplation carries the broader sense of pondering what something means. To ponder something is to quiet the mind, to clear the mind, to be set free from distractions in order to meditate on one thing. More narrowly, contemplation is the practice of relaxing attention, of quieting the mind in order to fully attend to what is paired together in the body of memory.

Together, meditation and contemplation convey the fruitfulness of examination as mindfulness, as attending and relaxing attention in the examination of what is known and not known in words, beyond words, and beyond one's particular life in the world. Such is the nature of consciousness as reflexive, as not simply drawing out the truth of something but of being drawn out in recognition of what claims a person and calls for response.

Meditation and contemplation are central to the particular exercises of the mind. These include oral conversations with others, reading texts, memorization, writing, dialogue with oneself, viewing things from the point of view of the cosmos, in terms of the order of action, as life lived unto death, and as being judged in one's life lived.

For Christians, meditation and contemplation are central to the reading and hearing of scripture and to prayer and worship. As in what has been called the divine reading of scripture (*lectio divina*), a phrase or line of scripture is read followed by silence so that attention is quieted to meditate on what is heard in memory. In prayer, attention is focused in praise and thanksgiving, in examination of oneself, in prayers for oneself, for others, and for the life of the world. In pause and silence, alongside of words prayed and sung, memory is broadened and deepened beyond what is prayed and sung. This is evident in remembering significant times in one's life and in the life of the world, at the birth of a child, in the celebration of a marriage, in the death and burial of a friend or a family member, in remembering the violence of war and in the celebration of peace. What is felt and known is beyond words but, nonetheless, is known in the body as remembered and in the play of images that form the memory of God.

Embodied Memory

Physical practices are spiritual as they examine and form the memory and awareness of the self in its availability and vulnerability, in its power and fragility, in its connectedness and its separateness. What are most often called ascetical practices, physical practices examine human desires in becoming indifferent toward indifferent things, and in knowing what is truly desired. For example, fasting, abstinence, and mortification of the body give rise to the feelings of hunger and the sense of our bodies as ourselves. Hunger calls attention in the present to our desires and needs and to memories of our dependence upon the gifts of creation and upon those who gather and prepare the food we eat and in all that we share together. Positioning the body and regulating breathing stills the body and focuses attention away from the distractions of sounds, sights, and smells, and from concerns over matters great and small. Silence for a moment or longer in retreat from daily life clears body and mind and opens the memory to what gives life.[16]

Moral Practices

Moral practices are likewise spiritual practices that attune the memory of the body in response to the powers and purposes that give life in the life of the world beyond oneself. Moral practices are not singular actions offered at a moment in time, such as helping someone who has fallen or lost one's way, sharing water with someone on a hot summer day, freeing a bird caught in a net, or giving a home to a feral cat. These may be moral acts, but they are not spiritual practices.

What makes moral practices Christian spiritual practices that form the memory of God is where what is done in act is done regularly paired in memory with the voices that form the Christian memory and call of God. And so, we speak of practices of hospitality, community service, the work of justice, and the care of creation, each as given in one's own time and place in the life of the world. In the practice of faith in believing, in worship as in life, in life as in worship, these are the memories of God heard singing the song of creation and redemption in the saving memory of God incarnate in the life of the world, in being in time as Father, Son, and Holy Spirit.

NOTES

1. On the history of the development of Christian churches, monastic communities, and the expansion of Christianity in the world of late antiquity, see Peter Brown, *The World of Late Antiquity, AD 150–750* (New York: W. W. Norton, 1989), esp. 49–112. For a comprehensive account of the more recent studies that have described the diversity of Christian communities, beliefs, and practices in late antiquity, see Peter Brown, *The Rise of Western Christendom: Triumph and Diversity A.D. 200–1000* (Oxford: Blackwell, 2003), 3rd edition. See especially his preface on the explosion of studies that form the distinct field of study, that of Late Antiquity, x–xlvii.

2. On the development and character of monastic life see Peter Brown, *The World of Late Antiquity*, especially 96–101; and Alexander Schmemann, *Introduction to Liturgical Theology*, tr. Asheleigh E. Moorehouse (Crestwood, NY: St. Vladimir's Seminary Press, 1966), 131–41.

3. *The Rule of Pachomius*, tr. G. H. Schodde (New York: T&T Clark, 1885), available online, https://westminsterabbey.ca/wp-content/uploads/2018/07/Pachomius-Rule-english.pdf; and The *Rule of St. Basil in Latin and English: A Revised Critical Edition*, tr. Anna M. Silvas. (Collegeville, MN: Liturgical Press, 2013); and in print and available online, E. F. Morison, tr. and introduction, *St. Basil and His Rule: A Study in Early Monasticism* (London: Oxford University Press. 1912.), online at https://www.academia.edu/42544425/ Saint Basil_and His_Rule_A Study_in Early Monasticism_E_F_Morrison.

4. *The Rule of St. Benedict* In English, tr. Timothy Fry, OSB (Collegeville, MN: Liturgical Press, 2019), available online. https://saintjohnsabbey.org/rule.

5. Schmemann, *Introduction to Liturgical Theology*, tr. Asheleigh Moorehouse (Crestwood, NY: St. Vladimir's Seminary Press, 1966), 141–44.

6. Bernard McGinn, *The Foundations of Mysticism: Origins to the Fifth Century* (New York: Crossroad Publishing,1991), 132.

7. Adolf von Harnack, *History of Dogma*, tr. Neil Buchanan (New York: Russell & Russell, 1958).

8. In addition to being at the source of the liturgical and ecumenical movements, the development of critical historical studies are central to the broader accounts of the history of Christianity and the nature of Christian faith. This is notably developed in Diarmaid MacCulloch's *Christianity: The First Three Thousand Years* (London: Penguin Books, 2009); see his discussion on "Canon, Creed, Ministry, Catholicity," 127–37, in chapter 5, "Boundaries Defined: (50 CE–300)," 114–54.

9. Schmemann, *Introduction to Liturgical Theology*, 131–45.

10. Pierre Hadot, *What Is Ancient Philosophy?* tr. Michael Chase (Cambridge, MA: The Belknap Press of Harvard University Press, 2002), 237–52. From his study of the writings of late antiquity and early Christianity, Michel Foucault's work provides the foundation for this turn to the hermeneutics of the self that is the focus of the understanding of Christian faith in this book. In describing the ways of interpreting how human persons come to understand themselves in acting in the world, Foucault moves from a focus on how power shapes truth claims that shape human intent and act to how human persons come to understand themselves in act in light of the shaping of desire in what he calls technologies of the self (or for Christians, that is to say "spiritual practices"). See Michel Foucault, *Ethics: Subjectivity and Truth, Essential Works of Foucault* 1954–1984), ed. Paul Rabinow, tr. Robert Hurley and others (New York: The New Press, 1997). See Rabinow's introduction on "The History of Systems of Thought," xi–xlii, and referenced writings. Also see *Technologies of the Self: A Seminar with Michel Foucault,* eds. Luther H. Martin, Huck Gutman, and Patrick H. Hutton (Amherst: The University of Masschusetts Press, 1988).

11. On the significance of women in forming Christian communities of faith in the patriarchal world of early Christianity, see Peter Brown, "Daughters of Jerusalem: The Ascetic Life of Women in The Fourth Century," *The Body and Society: Men, Women, and Sexual Renunciation in Early Christianity* (New York: Columbia University Press, 1988), 259–84.

12. Richard Norris, "What Are Bishops For?" *The Business of All Believers*, ed. Timothy F. Sedgwick (New York: Seabury, 2009), 97. Also see Hadot, on the sage, *What Is Ancient Philosophy?*, (Cambridge, MA: The Belknap Press of Harvard University Press, 2002), 220–52.

13. Pierre Hadot, *Philosophy as a Way of Life,* ed. Arnold I. Davidson, tr, Michael Case (Oxford: Blackwell, 1995), 84; and further chapter 3, "Spiritual Exercises, 81–125, and chapter 4, "Ancient Spiritual Exercises and 'Christian Philosophy,'" 126–44.

14. *Oxford English Dictionary*, from the Latin *exigere*.

15. Augustine, *Confessions: A New Translation*, tr. Sarah Ruden (New York: Modern Library, 2017), *Bk* I.1.

16. On the history and practices of asceticism as spiritual practice and as countercultural life identified with the presence and union with God, see. Vincent L. Wimbush and Richard Valantasis, *Asceticism* (Oxford: Oxford University Press, 2002). As practices past and present, see Richard Valantasis, *The Making of the Self: Ancient and Modern Asceticism* (Eugene, OR: Cascade Books, 2008).

Chapter Six

Church: One and Many

Lived out individually and corporately, the memory of God is passed on in Christian communities of worship. There the scaffolding of memory is formed in a polyphony of voices. However, the memory of God is narrowed, and the voice of God is muted, if not lost altogether, where prayer and worship and the practices of faith become reduced to a singular narrative rendering of the memory of God. Such is the nature of idolatry, or what Kenneth Kirk describes as the problem of formalism, rigorism, and institutionalism.[1]

FORMALISM, RIGORISM, INSTITUTIONALISM

As Aristotle speaks of human actions having both a formal cause and a material cause, the challenge and danger of formalism is where the material images of God and of life in God become narrowed to what is seen as the fulfillment of the life of the world and to what is thought to be required to enter the kingdom of God. The memory of God becomes an idea of human fulfillment in one's own life and way of life. Prayer and worship and the practices of faith become fidelity to the idea to be vigorously pursued to the end of time, which is to say, in fulfillment beyond challenge and change, diminishment, and loss. Until then, differences among people become matters of conflict over what is to be believed and done, differentiating those who are saved from those who are damned.

The idolatry of formalism and rigorism is not simply a matter of the individual. Formalism and rigorism arise institutionally where what is taught and required in worship and the practices of Cristian faith is regularized and regulated in the order of the church and society; in other words, in governing. Wedded together in formalism, rigorism, and institutionalism, Christian faith becomes a religion where beliefs are formulated in a creed and human fulfillment is understood and regulated in terms of a universal moral code, which, in turn, becomes a constant call effecting rigorism in act.

FAITH AND THE CHURCH

The challenge of formalism and rigorism came to the fore in the fourth century in what was to become the eastern Orthodox Church and the western Roman Catholic Church that, together, were to become the established Church of the Roman Empire. Institutionalized in an order of ministry with bishops as the ordained leaders of the Church as a communion of churches, the Church was established in worship and daily life as required of all, enforced by the power of the state in what we may call the "establishment account of Christian faith."[2]

As Wayne Meeks has written, toward the end of the second century, some Christians had come to think of Christian faith as tied to a canonically ordering of texts to form the Christian Bible of Old and New Testaments as a universal moral account of human history as part of cosmic time with beginning, middle, and end.[3] This is the history of the way of life and the way of death that reaches from the beginning of time in the conflict of good and evil, of order and chaos, as stories of fidelity and betrayal, of the rise and fall of kingdoms and empires, of heroes and villains, of saints becoming sinners and sinners becoming saints. The story of Jesus' life and teaching, death and resurrection represents the triumph of good over evil in the resurrection of the dead at the end of history.

This singular narrative account of salvation has been expressed as given in Word, sacrament, and ministry. This reflected the establishment of Christian scripture in the Christian Bible, the regularization of worship in liturgical rites centered in baptism and the Eucharist, and the development of leaders to govern the Church under the authority of bishops. Together the Church as a communion of churches was formed in life together in prayer and worship and the practices of Christian faith, including moral teachings of duties known and enforced in the examination of conscience and the sacrament of penance and reconciliation.

IN LIFE TOGETHER

And yet, while ordered in beliefs, prayer and worship, and spiritual practices, the memory of God was still given and heard in different memories of God arising in different times and places, past and present, addressing different challenges and questions. Still, Meeks claims, Christian faith and life are not "shapeless."[4] The moral drama of life in God heard together in the voices of many is the saving memory of what gives life together in time. This means, writes Meeks, that Christians "ought always to strive and pray for unity."

Practically, this leads Meeks to ask, "How much unity is achievable? How much diversity is tolerable?"[5] Born from the "large and often raucous diversity" of different Christian communities, Meeks concludes, "the unity that the one God gives is an eschatological gift."[6]

> We cannot wrest it into being in the land of unlikeness where human life is lived. Now, in the middle time, we have best not diminish too greatly our intellectual spiritual gene pool, our store of metaphors, stories, ideas, and institutions, but experimentation we need. Our creative polyphony needs the voices of some sects, some orders, some traditionalists, some experimental communities, some radical prophets.[7]

Faith in God is best understood in being one in life together in the memory of God in Christ, passed on from one generation to another, given the sins of the past and present, across cultures and societies, in response to new challenges and possibilities. This is the memory of God known and effected in the life of faith as life together in believing, in giving one's heart to God in remembrance in worship and the practices of faith, in acclamation and invocation, in thanksgiving and beseeching.

In the memory of God, through the waters of baptism and the laying on of hands, in the power of the Holy Spirit, the newly Baptized are received and incorporated (made one body) as members of the Church in life lived in giving themselves to the memory of God and in response to God in the life of the world. This is the memory of the body of God, of suffering the constraints and sins of the world paired in memory with the grace of new life in love that calls persons into life as one in many and many in one.

IN A SECULAR AGE

Freed from the constraints of the Church established by the state, Christian communities entered the secular age.[8] They were uprooted from their common life formed together in common prayer and worship and in the practices of Christian faith. Christian communities of faith have spiraled in different directions in response to different claims, challenges, and possibilities. New churches were formed in the reform of old churches and in the formation of new churches. These are in turn reformed within and apart in other new communities of religious faiths. Together, Christian denominations reflect a secular world rich in its diversity of cultures and communities, remembering and inventing, forming and reforming ways of life. Connected by a world economy, digital communications, and international travel, the world of Christian communities in the twenty-first century is deeply connected and deeply divided and falling apart.

Not unlike the world of Christian faith at the time of its birth during the rise of the Roman Empire, Christian communities are divided as the larger culture gives voice to the powers and purposes that are the meaning and values that rule the world in which they live. Increasingly the rendering of human life is imaged as the quest for the fulfillment of desire. The formal images of the human person are formed in terms of freedom and fulfillment.

This is an age of expressive individualism. The human person is imaged in terms of the autonomous self, the sovereign self, and the therapeutic self.[9] Roles and relations formed by the ritual practices of daily life no longer bind persons together in the memory of God. Memories of God and practices of faith and worship are as fragmented and discordant as are the voices and practices in a consumer world. Images of love and desire are torn from their mooring in time, as in the traditional pairing of such images as love and covenant, family and society, work and vocation.

In a secular world and consumer society, the memory and call of God is lost for many, if not most. Instead of calling persons into life together beyond themselves, the memory and call of God is captive to churches of the like-minded. Prayer and worship become a litany of their thanksgivings, hopes, and concerns. At the extreme, worship is turned into a platform for the politics of the like-minded, whether liberal or conservative in matters of church and society.

PROPHETIC VOICES

In a secular world and consumer society, as in any world, there are, of course, communities and individual persons juxtaposed to the idols of the age. Their lives and memories of life invite others into conversation about the powers and purposes that shape their lives, about what one knows and what one does not know, what are the possibilities for life well lived and fulfilled, and what makes it so.

In a secular age, some of the prophetic lives and voices will be Christian or have been formed from those who have themselves been formed in Christian communities. Others will have rejected altogether what they have experienced, remembered, or have been told of Christian faith and life. Most will, though, have roots reaching down into different communities and cultures, people and places. What they share is the call to life together beyond themselves. What they bear witness to is the prophetic memory of God and call of God at the heart of Christian faith.

INTO THE FUTURE

Christian communities will themselves be many, heirs of different histories and traditions, formed, reformed, transformed across generations, or born as new in different places with others in other cultures having their own rituals and spiritual practices. What they will share is the memory and call of God in life together formed in their own lives in the practices of Christian faith in Christian communities of worship. In turn, they will have leaders who have been formed in the practices of faith in Christian communities of worship. They will be people of God, holy in spirit, filled with the love of God, sharing in the life of the community together as companions, spiritual leaders, pastors, priests, teachers, ministers, presiding in life together in worship and life, in times of sorrow and joy, in lament and celebration, in thanksgiving and praise, in confession and beseeching, in gathering and sending, in life and in death.

NOTES

1. Kenneth Kirk, *The Vision of God,* 5–10, 466–72.
2. For an account of the formation and development of the Church as bearer of the memory of God institutionalized in the Roman Catholic Church, see Edward Schillebeeckx, *Church: The Human Story of God,* tr. John Bowden (New York: Crossroad Publishing Co., 1994). Offering a critical, ecclesiological theology, Schillebeeckx develops what is necessary for the order of governance in mediating the memory and call of God as known in life together in participation in the saving memory and call of God in the life of the world. As God incarnate, the memory and call of God, the divine and human, love of God and love of humankind, the mystical and the ethical, Christian faith and ethics are integral one to another in the life of the world, in being in time. See 91–101.
3. Wayne A. Meeks, *The Origins of Christian Morality: The First Two Centuries* (New Haven, CT: Yale University Press, 1993), 189–210.
4. Ibid., 216.
5. Ibid.
6. Ibid.
7. Ibid., 217.
8. Taylor, *A Secular Age* (Cambridge, MA: The Belknap Press of Harvard University Press, 2007), esp. part IV, "Narratives of Secularization," 423–535; and in *Dilemmas and Connections: Selected Essays* (Cambridge, MA: The Belknap Press of Harvard University Press, 2011), "What Does Secularism Mean?," 303–25; "Disenchantment-Reenchantment," 211–87; and "The Future of the Religious Past," 214–86.

9. *A Secular Age*, 473–75. Also, Charles Taylor, *Sources of the Self the Making of the Modern Identity* (Cambridge, MA: Belknap Press of Harvard University Press, 1989), 368–90.

Chapter Seven

Hallowed Be Thy Name

Memory attunes and calls us to respond in the life of the world. We believe in the memory of God in the actions of our lives. Together in memory and act we know the limitations, faults, and failures in our lives. We know the sins of the world that we bear in the life of the world. And in act we suffer the mystery of God and know the grace of love that gives life in life together.

Quoting Tertullian, the *Catechism of the Roman Catholic Church* says, quite simply, "The Lord's Prayer 'is truly the summary of the whole gospel.'"[1] As remembered as Jesus' prayer, which Jesus commends to his disciples (Matt. 6: 9–13, Lk. 11:1–13), the Lord's Prayer came to be prayed before communion as a prayer of devotion that is a summation of the Eucharist that is celebrated. As Gordon Lathrop says, "The Lord's Prayer, prayed as the last act of the thanksgiving at table, rightly sums up all our attempts at prayer and becomes, as it prays for God's bread and our mutual forgiveness, our best communion prayer."[2]

As the saving memory of God, the Lord's Prayer is not a summary of beliefs but bears the saving memory of God in prayer. In prayer, the words of the Lord's Prayer draw together the range of associations and meanings that those words have in a Christian community of faith. These memories are memories of times and places (social, cultural, economic, political, and more) that shape present memories, interests, and concerns. Memories of God are, moreover, shaped by participation together with others in the life and worship of Christian communities of worship.

The language of prayer and faith is polyphonic. In the community of faith at prayer and worship, scripture readings, prayers, psalms, hymns, homilies, and sermons draw on different images that complement one another and are juxtaposed one to another. The play of these images, given and enacted in prayer and worship and examined and deepened in the practices of faith, form the Christian "imaginary." In this sense, the Lord's Prayer draws together in prayer what is central to the saving memory of Christian faith.

Acclamation and Invocation

The Lord's Prayer has the form of a blessing.[3] Blessings are words of thanksgiving and beseeching. "What a blessed day this is." "Blessed are you." And then, "Bless this house, O Lord we pray, make it safe by night and day." Blessings acknowledge and give thanks for what is, and they give voice for a future "that it may be so." Other words convey these two sides of blessings. Praise is closely tied to giving thanks while beseeching is tied to praying for, asking for, petitioning, calling upon another. Blessings may be said to be two-fold: acclamation and invocation.

In the Lord's Prayer the acclamations and invocations (petitions) are connected. What is acclaimed about God claims what human life is to be. To pray to "our Father" is to claim that life is given together, in communion. This is underscored by the Aramaic word "abba," which is translated in the Greek, Latin, and English with what is now the more formal term, "father." Abba is, though, more akin to "papa." It is a term of intimacy. To pray to God as Father claims that God and humanity are related in life together as family.

From acclamations to invocations that it may be so, the memory of God central to Christian faith is also already and not yet. This is the memory of God that breaks open idols in the call to the newness of life that is love. Framed in the image of the kingdom of God as the eschaton, God breaks in upon our lives, as already and not yet.[4] And so, the Lord's Prayer calls all those who have ears to hear the call of God into the life of the world, not as their own but as God's, not as a program to be achieved but as a holy way of life in fidelity to the practices of faith centered in the worship of God. In acclamation and invocation, the Lord's Prayer attunes those have ears to hear to what gives life as the grace of God.

THE LORD'S PRAYER

In acclamation, the Lord's Prayer begins:

"Our Father in heaven, hallowed be thy name."

God above all creation, the power and order that is life. We paise you, honor you, and give ourselves to you whose name is "our Father."

"Your kingdom come, your will be done."

God is One, not in our imagination but in whatever will be.

"On earth as it is in heaven."

Incarnate in what is life, in what gives life in the time of our lives.

Paired with acclamation is invocation:
"Give us today our daily bread."

Food enough to eat, life together, welcoming one another, around a table to share, to rejoice and be glad. May it be so.

"Forgive us our debts, our trespasses, our sins as we forgive those who have sinned against us."[5]

May we forgive what we are owed, what has been done to us, and let go of the resentment that divides us, that in forgiving we may be forgiven and live in life together.

"Lead us not into temptation; save us from the time of trial."

May the memory of God be incarnate in our life together, that in compassion and care, in crucifixion and resurrection, may we in life incarnate love and rest together in the peace of God.

In a concluding doxology, in acclamation of praise:
"For yours is the kingdom, the power, and the glory, forever and ever. Amen."

THE ORDO OF FAITH

Prayed in the Lord's Prayer, formed and shaped in fidelity to the memory of God, Christian faith may be imaged as given together in the ordo of worship that is an ordo of devotion and the ordo of life. Together they celebrate and form life lived in the grace and love of God in the glory of creation in birth and death, in sickness and health, in compassion as one in another, in cross and resurrection. This awareness is the birth of moral conscience, of knowing that we do not know by ourselves what to do but hear in the voices of others what claims us and calls us to respond.

Attuned to the pathos of life and the call to respond, suffering the conflicts inherent in competing claims and possibilities, in faith, in humility and reverence, Christians respond in act that bears witness to the memory and call of God in the continuing conversion of life together that is the call of love. The Anglican divine Richard Hooker speaks of this memory of God as love and beauty. These two formal images—love and beauty—are paired as one.

The love of God gives voice to what forms life in time, to the beauty of God in creation. As in the difference between object and desire, between what is seen only through a glass darkly and the fulfillment of desire in act, beauty conveys the sense of being drawn out of ourselves in love of the life of the world in time. As Richard Hooker wrote in 1594,[6]

> Whereas we now love the thing that is good,
> but good especially in respect of benefit unto us;
> we shall then love the thing that is good, only or
> principally for the goodness of beauty in itself.

NOTES

1. *The Catechism of the Catholic Church,* 2nd ed. (Washington, DC: United States Conference of Catholic Bishops, 2016), sec. 2, art. 1, para. 2761, p. 662.

2 . Lathrop, *Saving Images,* 118.

3. *Saving Images,* on blessing, the Lord's Prayer, and the Eucharist, pp. 152–58.

4. On the eschatological character of the Lord's Prayer as structured in the parallelism of acclamation and invocation, see John Dominick Crossan, *The Greatest Prayer* (New York: HarperOne, 2010).

5. As remembered in the different memories of the Lord's Prayer expressed in what is to be forgiven by three different Greek words translated in English as debts (Matt. 6:12, Didache 8:2), as trespasses (Matt. 6:14–15), and as sins (Lk. 11:4).

6. Richard Hooker, *The Laws of Ecclesiastical Polity, Everyman's Library* (London: J. M. Dent & Sons, 1907), I.XII.3, p. 204.

Chronology

This chronology is drawn from comparative, scholarly dating of texts. On ancient philosophy and schools of philosophy, chronology has been drawn largely from Pierre Hadot, *What Is Ancient Philosophy?*, translated by Michael Chase (Cambridge, MA: Belknap Press of Harvard University Press, 2002), 330–41.

BCE—BEFORE THE COMMON ERA

435 +/-	Socrates teaches in Athens.
399	Death of Socrates
388/87	Plato forms his school called the Academy.
347	Death of Plato.
335	Aristotle forms his own school in Athens.
323	Death of Alexander the Great

HELLENISTIC PERIOD OF THE MEDITERRANEAN, BCE

306	Epicurus forms his school in Athens.
301	Zeno forms the Stoic school in Athens.
149–146	Macedonia and Greece submit to the Roman Republic.
106–43	Cicero, Roman statesman, philosopher influenced by the Academy. The schools founded by Plato, Aristotle, and Zeno disappear; schools founded by Epicurus survives; new schools of philosophy open.

THE ROMAN EMPIRE

27 BCE–14 CE	Caesar Augustus, First Roman Emperor

CE—THE COMMON ERA

29–30	Death of Jesus.
40 +/-	Death of Philo, Platonist philosopher important in the development of Hellenistic and early Christian writers.
54	Imperial Christian persecutions under Emperor Nero begin.
50–62	Composition of Pauline epistles
52–110	Chronologically from 1Thessolonians to 2Peter, texts written that were later agreed upon as Christian scripture including in the New Testament.
70–110	Composition of New Testament Gospels
80–120 +/-	*The Didache,* the oldest rule for a Christian community addressing Baptism, the eucharistic meal, and including the Lord's Prayer.
133 +/-	First Gnostic teacher, Basildes, in Alexandria.
140–367	Establishment of the canon of Christian scripture as Christian bible of Old and New Testaments.
150	*First Apology* of Justin Martyr (b. 100, d. 165).
180–230 +/-	*The Apostolic Tradition,* credited to Hippolytus (b. 217/218, d. 235), offering an account of church orders, the catechumenate, and moral rules regarding the life of churches.
180 ff	Development of schools in Alexandria and Caesarea as centers for teaching Christian thought informed by Platonism.
197	The *Apology* of Tertullian (b. 155, d. 240), including an account of the Eucharis.
185–254	Origen, educated in Alexandria, among the most significant of the first Christian apologists; through sermons, biblical interpretation, and theological treatises, offering an allegorical reading of scripture and a Neoplatonic account of Christian beliefs.
240–270	Plotinus forms a Neoplatonic school in Rome.
300 +/-	Beginning of Christian monasticism as solitary ascetics (anchorites, i.e., eremitic monks) "retire" to the desert in colonies of hermit shelters, remembered through Athanasius of Alexandria (b. 296/98, d. 373) writing of *The Life of Anthony* in 356 =/-.

THE CHRISTIAN EMPIRE

313	Emperor Constantine converts to Christianity and promulgates the Edict of Milan, providing toleration for Christians resulting in the establishment of the Roman Catholic Church.
325 +/-	The Rule of St. Pachomius indicating shared practices of life together in the first monastic communities (cenobitic monasticism) formed by Pachomius (b. 292, d. 348) along the Upper Nile in Egypt.
325	The Council of Nicea, the first ecumenical council of bishops.

360 ff	Church Fathers of "learned monasticism" and central to Eastern Orthodoxy, most notably the Cappadocian Fathers: Basil of Caesarea, aka Basil the Great (b. 330, d. 379); Gregory of Nazianzus (b. 329–d. 390); Gregory of Nyssa (b. 335, d. 395); and John Chrysostom (b. 347, d. 407).
366 +/-	The Rule of St. Basil (that became with the Rule of St. Pachomius the two originating rules of cenobitic monastic communities.
380	Edict of Thessalonica. Emperor Theodosius establishes Christianity as the religion of the Roman Empire.
381	First Council of Constantinople, Second Ecumenical Council, adopted Nicene–Constantinopolitan Creed that liturgically became designated as the Nicene Creed, accepted by the major churches of Eastern, Oriental, and Western Christianity.
386–430	Writings of Augustine (b. 354, d. 430) as the most influential theologian of the Western Church. Other prominent, early Latin Fathers (teachers) include Ambrose (b. 340, d. 397) and Jerome (b. 347, d. 420).
476	Fall of Rome
516	The Rule of Benedict

Bibliography

Altieri, Charles. *The Particulars of Rapture: An Aesthetics of the Affects.* Ithaca, NY: Cornell University Press, 2003.

Augustine. *Confessions.* Translated by Sarah Ruden. New York: The Modern Library, 2018.

Baldovin, John. "Eucharistic Prayer." *The New Westminster Dictionary of Liturgy & Worship.* Edited by Paul Bradshaw. Louisville: Westminster John Knox Press, 2002, 192–99.

Barber, Michael. "Alfred Schutz," *The Stanford Encyclopedia of Philosophy.* Spring 2014 Edition, http://plat.stanford.edu/archives/spr2014/ entries/schutz/.

Barth, Karl. *The Epistle to the Romans.* Translated by Edwin C. Hoskyns. London: Oxford, 1933.

Basil the Great. The Rule of St. Basil in Latin and English. A Revised Critical Edition. Translated by Anna M. Silvas. Collegeville, MN: Liturgical Press, 2013.

Bellah, Robert N. *Religion in Human Evolution.* Cambridge, MA: Belknap Press of Harvard University Press, 2011.

Bonhoeffer, Dietrich. *Psalms: The Prayer Book of the Bible.* Minneapolis, MN: Augsburg, 1970.

Bradshaw, Paul. *The New Westminster Dictionary of Liturgy & Worship.* Edited by Paul Bradshaw. Louisville, KY: Westminster John Knox, 2002.

Bradshaw, Paul, et. al. "Daily Prayer," in *The New Westminster Dictionary of Liturgy & Worship.* Edited by Paul Bradshaw. Louisville, KY: Westminster John Knox, 2002, 140–59.

Brown, Peter. *The Body and Society: Men, Women and Sexual Renunciation in Early Christianity.* New York: Columbia University Press, 1988.

———. *The World of Late Antiquity.* New York: Norton, 1989.

———. *The Rise of Western Christendom: Triumph and Diversity A.D. 200–1000.* Oxford: Blackwell, 2003, 3rd ed.

Brueggemann, Walter, and William Bellinger, Jr. *Psalms: New Cambridge Bible Commentary.* New York: Cambridge University Press, 2014.

———. Theology of The Old Testament: Testimony, Dispute, Advocacy. Minneapolis, N: Fortress Press, 2nd ed., 2005.

———. *Praying the Psalms.* Eugene, OR: Cascade Books, 2007.

Bryan, Christopher, ed. *Essays on "The Formation of Conscience." Sewanee Theological Review* 62(Pentecost 2019) 3: 433–614.
Crossan, John Dominic. *The Dark Interval.* Niles, IL: Argus, 1975.
———. *The Greatest Prayer.* New York: HarperOne, 2010.
———. *In Parables.* New York: Harper & Row, 1973.
———. *Raid on the Articulate.* New York: Harper Row, 1976.
Culler, Johnathan. "Lyric, History, and Genre," *The Lyric Theory. Reader.* Edited by Virginia Jackson and Yopie Prins. Cambridge, MA: Harvard University Press, 2015, 63–77.
Deacon, Terrence W. *Incomplete Nature: How Mind Emerged from Matter.* New York: W. W. Norton, 2013.
———. *The Symbolic Species: The Co-evolution of Language and the Brain.* New York: W. W. Norton, 1997.
Didache. Translated and commentary by Aaron Milavec. Collegeville, MN: Liturgical Press, 2003.
Didache. Translated by J. B. Lightfoot. Early Christian Writings. Online at https://www.earlychristianwritings.com, ch, 9–10.
Dix, Dom Gregory. *The Shape of the Liturgy.* New York: Seabury, 1982; 1st ed., 1945.
Donald, Merlin. *A Mind So Rare: The Evolution of Human Consciousness.* New York: Norton, 2001.
———. *Origins of the Modern Mind.* Cambridge, MA: Harvard University Press, 1991.
Foucault, Michel. *Ethics: Subjectivity and Truth, Essential Works of Foucault 1954–1984.* Edited by Paul Rabinow. Translated by Robert Hurley and others. New York: The New Press, 1997.
———. *Technologies of the Self.* Edited by L. Martin, H. Gutman, and P. Hutton. Amherst, MA: University of Massachusetts Press, 1988.
Goethe, Johann Wolfgang von. *Faust.* The Project Gutenberg EBook of Faust, 2007. J. Studirzimmer, lines 47–60. Online at gutenberg.org/files/21000/2100-h/21000-h.htm.
Guroian, Vigen. "Love That Is Divine and Human," *The Orthodox Reality: Culture, Theology, and Ethics in the Modern World.* Grand Rapids, MI: Baker Academic, 2018, 107–22.
Hadot, Pierré. *Philosophy as a Way of Life: Spiritual Exercises from Socrates to Foucault.* Edited and introduction, Arnold I. Davidson. Translated by Michael Chase. Oxford: Blackwell, 1995.
———. *What Is Ancient Philosophy?* Translated by Michael Chase. Cambridge, MA: The Belknap Press of Harvard University Press, 2002.
Haugeland, John. *Dasein Disclosed: John Haugeland's Heidegger.* Edited by Joseph Rouse. Cambridge, MA: Harvard University Press, 2013.
Heidegger, Martin. *Being and Time. Translated by* John Macquarrie and Edward Robinson. Oxford: Blackwell, 1962.
———. "Letter on Humanism," *Martin Heidegger: Basic Writings.* Ed, David Farrell Krell. Translated by Frank A. Capuzzi. London: Harper Perennial, 2008, 217–265.

———. "Poetically Man Dwells." Translated by Albert Hofstadter. *The Lyric Theory Reader: A Critical Anthology. Eds.* Virginia Jackson and Yopie Prins. Baltimore: Johns Hopkins University Press, 2014), 390–99.

Hooker, Richard. *Of the Laws of Ecclesiastical Polity. Everyman's Library.* London: J. M. Dent & Sons, 1907.

Illich, Ivan. *The Rivers North of the Future: The Testament of Ivan Illich as told to David Cayley.* Edited by David Cayley. Toronto, Canada: House of Anansi Press, 2005.

Jackson, Virginia and Yopie Prins, eds. *The Lyric Theory Reader: A Critical Anthology.* Baltimore: Johns Hopkins University Press, 2014.

———. "Phenomenology of Lyric Reading." In *The Lyric Theory Reader: A Critical Anthology.* Baltimore: Johns Hopkins University Press, 2014, 382–89.

Justin, *1 Apology* 67. Translated by Gordon W. Lathrop, *Holy Things, A, Liturgical Theology.* Minneapolis, MN: AugsburgFortress, 1993, 45.

Kandel, Eric R. *In Search of Memory: The Emergence of a New Science of Mind.* New York: W. W. Norton, 2006.

Kauffman, Stuart. *At Home in the Universe: The Search for the Laws of Self-organization and Complexity.* New York: Oxford University Press, 1995.

Kavanagh, Aidan. *On Liturgical Theology.* New York: Pueblo, 1984.

———. *The Shape of Baptism: The Rite of Christian Initiation.* New York: Pueblo, 1978.

Keller, Hellen with Anne Sullivan and John A. Macy. *The Story of My Life.* New York: Doubleday, 1903.

Kierkegaard, Søren. *Fear and Trembling.* Translated by Walter Lowrie. Princeton, NJ: Princeton University Press, 2013.

Kirk, Kenneth. *The Vision of God.* London: Longmans, Green and Co., 1932.

Kohák, Erazim. *The Embers and the Stars: A Philosophical Inquiry into the Moral Sense of Nature.* Chicago: The University of Chicago Press, 1984.

Lathrop, Gordon H. *Holy People: A Liturgical Ecclesiology.* Minneapolis, MN: Fortress, 1999.

———. *Holy Things: A Liturgical Theology.* Minneapolis, MN: Fortress, 1993.

———. *Saving Images: The Presence of the Bible in Christian Liturgy.* Minneapolis, MN: Fortress, 2017.

Lift Every Voice and Sing II: An African American Hymnal. New York: Church Publishing, 1993.

Lewis, Harold T. "Introduction: Why an African American Hymnal?" *Lift Every Voice and Sing II: An African American Hymnal.* New York: Church Publishing, 1993, xii–xvi.

Logan, Robert K. "The Terrance Deacon's Incomplete Nature: How Mind Emerged from Matter: A Review and Précis of *An Incomplete Nature." ETC: A Review of General Semantics* 71 (Oct. 2014) 4: 301–323. https://www.jstor.org/stable/24761945.

Luther, Martin. "Preface to the Psalter." *Luther's Works,* Edited by E. Theodore Backman. Philadelphia: Muhlenberg, 1960. Vol. 35.

Mariscal, Carlos, et al. Workshop Report: "Hidden Concepts in the History and Philosophy of Origins-of-Life Studies. Review of Current Literature on What

Is Described as the Science of Mind." In A *History of Philosophy of Origin of Life Studies*. Published online at Origins of Life and Evolution of Biospheres 09 August, 2019. Pp. 1–35. Nature B.V. © Springer 2019. https://link.springer.com /article/10.1007/s11084-019-09580-x Accessed 10.31.19.

Maurice, F. D. *The Kingdom of Christ.* 2 vols. Edited by Alex R. Vidler. London: SCM Press, 1958, 2nd ed. 1842.

MacCulloch, Diarmaid. *Christianity: The first Three Thousand Years*. London: Penguin Books, 2009.

McGinn, Bernard. *The Foundations of Mysticism: Origins to the fifth century.* New York: Crossroad, 1991.

Mead, George Herbert. *Mind, Self, and Society.* Chicago: University of Chicago Press, 1934.

Meeks, Wayne A. The *Origins of Christian Morality: The First Two Centuries*. New Haven. CT: Yale University Press, 1993.

Morison, E. F. Translated by and introduction, *St. Basil and His Rule: A Study in Early Monasticism*. London: Oxford University Press. 1912. Online at https://www.academia.edu/42544425/Saint_Basil_and_His_Rule_A_Study_in _EarlyMonasticism_E_F_Morrison.

Nabert, Jean. *Elements for an Ethic*. Translated by Paul Ricoeur and William J. Petrek. Evanston, IL: Northwestern University Press, 1969.

Niebuhr, H. Richard. *Radical Monotheism and Western Culture, With Supplementary Essays.* Louisville, KY: Westminster/John Knox, 1943, 1952, 1955, 1960.

———. *The Kingdom of God in America.* Chicago: Willet, Clark & Co., 1937.

———. *The Meaning of Revelation.* New York: Macmillan, 1941.

———. *The Responsible Self: An Essay in Christian Moral Philosophy.* New York: Harper & Row, 1963.

———. *The Social Sources of Denominationalism.* Cleveland, OH: Meridian Books, 1929.

Norris, Richard. "What Are Bishops For?" *The Business of All Believers*. Edited by Timothy F. Sedgwick. New York: Seabury, 2009.

Ojakangas, Mika. *The Voice of Conscience: A Political Genealogy of Western Ethics Experience.* New York: Bloomsbury, 2013.

Osiek, Carolyn Ann, and David L. Balch. *Families in the New Testament World: Households and House Churches.* Philadelphia: Westminster/John Knox, 1997.

Pachomius. *The Rule of Pachomius.* Translated by G. H. Schudde. Aeterna Press, 2014; 1st ed. London T & T Clark, 1885. First ordinance; available online at https: //westminsterabbey.ca/wp-content/uploads/2018/07/Pachomius-Rule-english.pdf<.

Pecklers, Keith F. et al. "The Liturgical Movement." In *The New Westminster Dictionary of Liturgy and Worship*. Edited by Paul Bradshaw. Louisville, KY: Westminster John Knox, 2002.

Perrin, Norman. *Gospel and Parables.* Minneapolis, MN: AugsburgFortress, 2003.

Plato. *Apology, The Dialogues of Plato.* Translated by Benjamin Jowett. New York: Random House, 1937.

Rappaport, Roy A. *Ritual and Religion in the Making of Humanity.* Cambridge: Cambridge University Press, 1999.

Ricoeur, Paul. *Hermeneutics: Writings and Lectures, Vol. 2.* Translated by David Pellauer. Cambridge, UK: Polity Press, 2013.

———. "Nabert on Act and Sign." Edited by Don Ihde. The Conflict of Interpretation: Essays in Hermeneutics. Evanston, IL: Northwestern University Press, 1974, 211–35.

———. *The Rule of Metaphor.* Translated by Robert Czerny. Toronto: University of Toronto Press, 1977.

———. Saliers, Don E. *Worship as Theology.* Nashville, TN: Abingdon, 1994.

Schillebeeckx, Edward. *Church: The Human Story of God.* Translated by John Bowden. New York: Crossroad Publishing Co., 1994.

Schmemann, Alexander. *Introduction to Liturgical Theology.* Translated by Asheleigh Moorehouse. Crestwood, NY: St. Vladimir's Seminary Press, 1966.

———. "Worship in a Secular Age," For the Life of the World: Sacraments and Orthodoxy. Crestwood, NY: St. Vladimir's Seminary Press,1963, 117–34.

Schutz, Alfred. *Collected Papers* I. Edited by Maurice Natanson. The Hague: Martinus Nijhoff, 1971.

———. *Collected Papers II: Studies in Social Theory.* Edited by Arvid Brodersen. The Hague: Martinus Nijhoff,1964.

———. *The Phenomenology of the Social World.* Translated by George Walsh and Frederick Lehnert. Evanston, IL: Northwestern University Press, 1967.

Schweitzer, Albert. *Reverence for Life.* Translated by Reginald H. Fuller. New York: Harper & Row, 1969.

Sedgwick, Peter H. *The Origins of Anglican Moral Theology.* Leiden: Brill, 2019.

———. *The Development of Anglian Moral Theology, 1680–1950.* Leiden: Brill, 2024.

Sedgwick, Timothy F. "The Anglican Exemplary Tradition." *Anglican Theological Review* 94 (Spring 2012) 2:207–231.

———. *The Christian Moral Life: Practices of Piety.* Grand Rapids, MI: Eerdmans, 1999; republished Seabury Press, 2008.

———. "Conscience and the Voice of God." *Sewanee Theological Review* 62 (Pentecost 2019) 3:459–77.

———. *Sacramental Ethics: Pascal Identity and the Christian Life.* Philadelphia: Fortress Press, 1987.

———. "The Trajectory of Christian Mission." *Church, Society and the Christian Common Good: Essays in Conversation with Philip Turner.* Edited by Ephraim Radner. Eugene, OR: Cascade Books, 2017, 34–42.

———. "Vision and Collaboration: Roland Allen, Liturgical Renewal, and Ministry Development." *Anglican Theological Review*, 2000, 8(1):155–71.

Silvas, Anna M. *The Rule of St Basil in Latin and English: A Revised Critical Edition.* Collegeville, MN: Liturgical Press, 2013.

Sinard, Suzanne. *Finding the Mother Tree.* New York: Alfred A. Knopf, 2021.

Smith, Dennis E. *From Symposium to Eucharist: The Banquet in the Early Christian World.* Minneapolis, MN: Fortress, 2003.

Stern, Daniel N. *Diary of a Baby.* New York: Basic Books, 1990.

———. *The Interpersonal World of the Infant.* New York: Basic Books, 1985.
Taylor, Charles. *A Secular Age.* Cambridge, MA: Belknap Press of Harvard University Press, 2007.
———. *Dilemmas and Connections: Selected Essays.* Cambridge, MA: The Belknap Press of Harvard University Press, 2011.
———. "Disenchantment-Reenchantment," *Dilemmas and Connections: Selected Essays.* Cambridge, MA: The Belknap Press of Harvard University Press, 2011: 287–302.
———. "The Future of the Religious Past," *Dilemmas and Connections: Selected Essays.* Cambridge, MA: The Belknap Press of Harvard University Press, 2011, 214–86.
———. "What Does Secularism Mean?," *Dilemmas and Connections: Selected Essays.* Cambridge, MA: The Belknap Press of Harvard University Press, 2011, 303–25.
———. *Sources of the Self: The Making of the Modern Identity.* Cambridge, MA: Belknap Press of Harvard University Press, 1989.
The Anglican-Roman Catholic Theological Consultation in the U.S.A., ARC-USA. "Ecclesiology and Moral Discernment: Seeking a Unified Moral Witness." Online at the website for The United States Conference of Catholic Bishops. Search for ecclesiology-and-moral-discernment-seeking a unified moral witness arcusa-2014-statement (1).pdf.
The *Book of Common Prayer.* New York: Church Publishing, 1978.
The Rule of St. Benedict, in English. Translated by Timothy Fry, OSB. Collegeville, MN: Liturgical Press, 2019, Available online. https://saintjohnsabbey.org/rule.
Verhey, Allen. *Remembering Jesus: Christian Community, Scripture, and the Moral Life.* Grand Rapids, MI: Eerdmans, 2002.
Wall, John. *Moral Creativity: Paul Ricoeur and the Poetics of Possibility.* New York: Oxford University Press, 2005.
Wheeler, Michael. "Martin Heidegger." *The Stanford Encyclopedia of Philosophy.* Edited by Edward N. Zalta. Winter 2018 Edition. 2.2.7; https://plato.stanford.edu/archives/win2018/entries/Heidegger/.
Wolfe, Judith. *Heidegger and Theology.* London: Bloomsbury, 2014.
Woodruff, Paul. *Reverence: Renewing a Forgotten Virtue.* New York: Oxford University Press, 2001.

Index of Biblical Texts

New Testament Texts

Matthew
    6:9–13   63
    13:31–32   2
    19:21   47
    26:26–29   24
    28:18, 19   28

Mark
    14:22   24

Luke
    1:46–55   23
    1:68–79   23
    1:51–53   23
    1:71, 79   23
    2:29, 31, 32   23
    10:25–37   1
    11:1–13   63
    15:11–31   1
    17:33   3
    22:15–20   24
    23:45   40

John
    1:1–4   25
    1:1–18   24
    1:14, 18   25
    1:9, 12   25
    6:32, 35   25
    13:4–12   24
    14: 27   24
    15:1   25
    15:4, 5, 9–11   25
    15:12–13   24
    20:19–23   26
    21:15–17   26

1 Corinithians
    11:23–26   24
    13:4–8   2

Galatians
    5:20–23   43

1 John
    4:8, 16   2

Philippians
    2:7   40

Old Testament Texts

Genesis
    1:1   27
    2:4–3, 24   37
    12–22   37

Index of Biblical Texts

34:24–29	38	

Deuteronomy
   5:7, 8   23

Ecclesiastes
   1:2   37

Exodus
   3:1–15   38
   3:14   38
   20:3–4   23

Isaiah
   6:1–5   38
   43:18–19   24
   49:6   23

Job
   2:10   22

1 Kings
   9:11–12   38

Psalms
   62   22

Index of Names

Aristotle, 57
Augustine, 51

Barth, Karl, 29
Basil of Caesarea, 47–48
Bonhoeffer, Dietrich, 22
Brueggemann, 28

Deacon, Terrence, 14–16
Dix, Gregory, 38–40

Goethe, 25

Harnack, Adolph von, 49
Heidegger, Martin, 4–5
Hooker, Richard, 65, 66

Johnson, James Weldon, 42
Justin, 35–36

Kandel, Eric, 13–15
Kant, Immanuel, 16
Kavanagh, Aidan, 29, 39, 40
Keller, Helen, 11–13, 17
Kierkegaard, Søren, 29

Kohák, Erazim, 5–6

Lathrop, Gordon, 39–40, 63
Luther, Martin, 22

McGinn, Bernard, 48–49
Maurice, F.D., 29
Meeks, Wayne, 58–59

Niebuhr, H.R., 27, 29,
Norris, Richard, 50

Pachomius, 47
Philo of Alexandria, 50
Plato, 3, 6–7
Prosper of Aquitaine, 33

Saliers, Don, 40
Schmemann, 39, 40
Socrates, 3–7
Stern, Daniel, 9–10

Taylor, Charles, 5
Tertulian, 63

Index of Subjects

baptism and Eucharist, 39, 49
Book of Psalms, 21–23

canticles, 23
    Benedictus Dominus Deus, Lk. 1:68–79
    The Magnificat, Lk. 1:46–55
    Nunc Dimittis, Lk. 2:22:29
Church:
    as established, 41
    formed in the Roman Empire, 47–50
    house churches, 34–35
    monastic communities, 48–50
conscience:
    Socrates and Plato, 3–4
    Voice of God, 3–4
    See also Moral Consciousness

Didache, 27

faith and believing, 28–29, 40, 49, 59
formalism, rigorism, institutionalism, 57–58

God is love, 2

idolatry, 29, 57
image of God, 21:
    incarnate, 24
    logos, 24–25
    personal images, 27
    the Trinity, 27–28
    YHWH, 38
    See also the Memory of God

Lord's Prayer, 63–65
love of God, 40, 6,
love and beauty, 66
lyric voice, 25–26

memory:
    development of, 9–13
    language development, 11–12, 16–18
    Helen Keller, 11–13, 17
    neurobiology, 13–15
    as symbolic, 16–18
    as teleodynamic, 15–16
memory of God, 17, 21, 34:
    in creation and redemption, 25, 30, 36–37
    in different voices, 8, 58
    Eucharistic memory, 34–43
    in the Lord's Prayer, 63–65
    as a new song, 23–24
    in prophetic voices, 23, 24, 37, 60, 41, 42

in sin and salvation, 37
  in time, 23, 24, 37–38, 58
  See also the Shape of the Liturgy
monastic communities:
  early monastic communities,
    47–49
  monastic rules and practices, 48,
    53–54
  as a renewal movement, 48–49
  See also Spiritual Practices
moral consciousness:
  as attunement, 4–5
  care and concern, 4
  doubt and questioning, 3–4
  and moral judgment, 5
  as originary, 6
  Plato and Socrates, 3–4, 6–7

neo-orthodoxy, 29
Nicene Creed, 29

parables, 1–2
polyphony, 21–23, 26–27, 38

radical monotheism, 29

scaffolding of memory, 16–18, 21, 28
a secular age, 5, 59–61
shape of the liturgy:
  earliest Eucharistic prayers, 34–35
  images of the shape, 38–41
  lex orandi lex credendi, 33–34
spiritual practices, 50–51
  ascetic practices, 52
  early list of practices, 50
  of the mind, 51–52
  moral practices, 52–53

worship as ritual, 34

About the Author

Timothy F. Sedgwick is the Clinton S. Quin Professor Emeritus of Christian Ethics at Virginia Theological Seminary. His teaching, writings, and service to the church have focused on what it is to be the people of God centered together as a community of worship and what that means in the life of the Church and in the life of the world. Among his books published are *Sacramental Ethics* (1987), *The Christian Moral Life* (1999), and *Sex, Moral Teaching, and the Unity of the Church* (2014).